ESS

Denmark

by
JUDITH SAMSON

Judith Samson once worked in the Foreign Office and
has travelled extensively. More recently, she has been
involved in research, writing and editing of
guidebooks and magazines.

Produced by AA Publishing

Written by Judith Samson
Verified by Judith Samson
Peace and Quiet section
by Paul Sterry

Revised second edition 1997
Reprinted 1995
First published 1993

Edited, designed and produced
by AA Publishing.
© The Automobile Association
Maps © The Automobile Association

Distributed in the United Kingdom
by AA Publishing, Norfolk House,
Priestley Road, Basingstoke,
Hampshire, RG24 9NY.

A CIP catalogue record for this
book is available from the British
Library.

ISBN 0 7495 1329 2

Published by AA Publishing, a
trading name of Automobile
Association Developments Limited,
whose registered office is Norfolk
House, Priestley Road, Basingstoke,
Hampshire, RG24 9NY.

Registered number 1878835.

Colour separation: BTB Colour
Reproduction Ltd, Whitchurch,
Hampshire

Printed by: Printers S.R.L., Trento,
Italy

Front cover picture: *Hans Christian
Andersen's Little Mermaid,
Copenhagen*

Country Distinguishing Signs

On the maps, international signs have been used to indicate the
location of the countries which surround Denmark.
Thus:
Ⓓ is Germany
Ⓢ is Sweden

Contents

Vor Frelsers Kirke

Years of Turmoil

Religious and political divisions culminated in the Thirty Years War (1618–48) which ravaged much of central Europe. Sweden battled it out with Denmark and regained most of its provinces, except Bornholm and Denmark's remaining provinces in Norway.

In 1660 King Frederik III deprived the nobility of their privileges and proclaimed himself absolute monarch. He reorganised the country's defences, but the wars with Sweden continued intermittently until 1720.

Much of the 18th century was marked by social advancements such as granting civil rights to the peasants and allowing them to buy or rent land, but although Denmark had acted ahead of international political developments, such as the French Revolution, it nevertheless became caught up in the Napoleonic Wars that followed. As a result, Britain restricted the maritime freedom of neutral nations, and as Denmark had signed a treaty of armed neutrality with other Baltic powers, the British sent an expedition, led by Nelson in 1801, which forced Denmark to withdraw. Six years later Copenhagen was bombarded by another British fleet; Denmark was forced to side with Napoleon who threatened to invade Jutland. Sweden's reward for joining the enemies of France was that Norway should be ceded to Sweden – which it was – under the Treaty of Kiel (1814).

Constitutional Change

In 1849 Denmark became a constitutional monarchy when King Frederik VII handed over most of his power to a two-chamber

The Golden Age

The 19th century was, for Denmark, dominated by the rise of Prussia, but internally there was a period of peace which allowed the arts to thrive. The years 1810–48 were considered the Golden Age of Danish art, when sculptor Bertel Thorvaldsen, writer Hans Christian Andersen, philospher Søren Kirkegaard, educationalist N F S Grundtvig, and numerous painters, including Eckersberg and Købke, flourished.

BACKGROUND

On duty

parliament, making the country a very democratic one for its time.

The struggles in the south of Jutland continued: Schleswig (which was Danish) did not trust the new constitution and asked to be united with Holstein, already in the German Confederation. Bismarck, the Prussian prime minister, declared war and Denmark lost Schleswig in 1864 – a situation which was to last 56 years – but the population retained the Danish language.

By the end of the 19th century, several political parties had come into being and the ideas of revolutionary socialism had begun to percolate through society: industrialisation got under way, helped by the newly built railways and trade unions were formed. Danish farmers switched from grain to dairy products and bacon, and created cooperatives, helping pave the way to their political power.

The new royal family grew into the unpretentious monarchy which is so well known today. Elections in 1901 led to the first democratic government, and the old aristocratic Denmark faded in 1915 when the electoral privileges of the upper chamber of parliament were removed and women were given the vote. World War I found Denmark neutral – the Battle of Jutland was fought off the north Danish coast. As a result of a post-war plebiscite, the people of Schleswig voted to return to Denmark and Iceland became an independent sovereign state.

A generation later the country was not so fortunate: Denmark was invaded in 1940 by Hitler's forces, but a strong resistance movement arose which sabotaged factories and saved thousands of Jews.

Post-war Denmark

After the war, closer ties developed with other Scandinavian countries and Denmark was a founder member of EFTA (European Free Trade Association). Today it belongs to the Nordic Council, NATO and the EU (which Greenland left in 1985).

Denmark has a popular monarchy, headed by Queen Margrethe II, who is married to Prince Henrik. Their sons are Crown Prince Frederik and Prince Joachim, who married Alexandra

Manley in 1995. The current government is a minority coalition of the Social Democrats, Social Liberals and Centre Democrats. Nine parties gained seats in the 179-seat Folketing (Parliament) which includes two members from Greenland and two from the Faroe Islands. Denmark, with a population of just over 5 million, is one of the most prosperous countries in the world, with a very high standard of living. The widespread provision of nursery schools caters for the high proportion of families with two wage earners.

The country's most serious problems now are the large national debt and the relatively high level of unemployment, currently around 10 per cent. To pay for its generous welfare services, taxation levels are high. Whatever the family income, all children receive an allowance. Pensions are paid to those aged 67 and over, but early retirement is possible. Manufacturing industries account for about a third of Danish production, (food, beverages, metal products) with agriculture and fisheries accounting for only about 6 per cent. Not surprisingly, Denmark strongly supports the EU's new liberal trade policies. It cares keenly about the environment and was the first country in Europe to appoint a Ministry of the Environment, whose wide brief includes protecting nature, controlling pollution and the preservation of ancient buildings.

A Fanø toddler in traditional bonnet

Tourists will be impressed by the cleanliness of the towns and though many older cities were ravaged by fire, their few surviving wooden buildings are often beautifully restored. Most towns have a similar layout with an industrial area and parking facilities on the outskirts. The town centre is likely to be dominated by a well-maintained church and close by will be a market square (with markets on Wednesdays and Saturdays), perhaps a small cluster of half-timbered houses in an area of old cobbled streets, a local museum (often free entry) and a pedestrian shopping area.

This apparent uniformity makes it easy for tourists. Driving through Denmark, visitors will be surprised at how well hidden the industry is, giving the impression that this is still primarily an agricultural economy.

What to See

COPENHAGEN (KØBENHAVN)

Colourful and clean, friendly and fashionable, Copenhagen is a lively and compact city which is easy to explore. If you are used to walking about 5 miles (8km) a day it is best covered on foot – otherwise, you will need to take buses. For example, it is nearly 2 miles (3km) from the station to Rosenborg Palace and half a mile (1km) from the main hotel area to the Town Hall. Copenhagen was the first city in Europe to ban cars and the mile-long (1.6km) **Strøget** (pronounced Stroit), is a pedestrian street (actually five streets) where no cars have been driven since 1962. Copenhagen's architecture ranges from medieval brick buildings along winding streets to modern glass blocks beside six-lane highways. The inner city is clearly defined, and is divided by Strøget, running from the newly paved **Rådhuspladsen** (Town Hall Square) in the west to **Kongens Nytorv** (the King's New Square) in the east. The oldest area is

around Strøget and includes the shady, cobbled square of Gråbrødretorv.
If it's hot you can stroll through one of the numerous parks or relax in an outdoor café and be entertained by youthful buskers, or you could take a waterside walk, perhaps to the famous, rather wistful statue of **den lille Havfrue** (the Little Mermaid). Copenhagen has a small canal network and a large harbour, but it's easy to forget that the city is by the sea until you suddenly come upon a forest of masts on **Nyhavn** canal. This was dug 300 years ago to encourage boats to sail nearer the city centre.
Apart from the parks, there are some lovely gardens – the large and tree-filled **Botanisk Have** (Botanical Gardens), and the delightful walled garden of the recently extended **Royal Library**. Some of Copenhagen's attractive monuments include the seated figure of **Hans Christian Andersen** and the **Lurblowers** outside the Palace Hotel. The huge **Gefion fountain**, near the Mermaid, depicts her four sons turned into oxen.

Getting your Bearings
Take a city bus tour (HT Sightseeing lets you get on and off at nine stops), or better still, take a canal boat starting from Gammel Strand or Nyhavn (guided tours) or the Water Bus (from Nyhavn, no guide), which stops at major sights. A new tour to the old Holmen naval station starts from Holmens Kirke. For a bird's-eye view climb:
- the dome of Marmorkirken
- the outside staircase of Vor Frelsers Kirke
- to the viewing platform of Rundetårn (Round Tower)
- the tower of the Rådhus (Town Hall)
- to the roof terrace of Illum.

History

Copenhagen began as a small fishing village (*havn*) where the herring industry provided the main source of income. In the 12th century King Valdemar the Great handed 'Havn' to Bishop Absalon of Roskilde, then the main city in Denmark, who built a fortress on Slotsholmen island to keep away marauding raiders. (Today the remains can be seen under Christiansborg Palace.) Over the next 200 years the town grew and became an important commercial centre, known as Købmands Havn (Merchants' Harbour), owned alternately by the king and the bishops. Erik of Pomerania imposed a toll on ships passing through the Øresund to increase the city's prosperity. Copenhagen became the capital city in 1443. Between 1600 and 1650, the city almost doubled in size when Christian IV, the 'Builder King', created the canal area of Christianshavn and also bought land to the northeast to build his castles. His green-spired buildings remain an attractive legacy, but his extravagance impoverished the city.

Gefion and her transformed sons

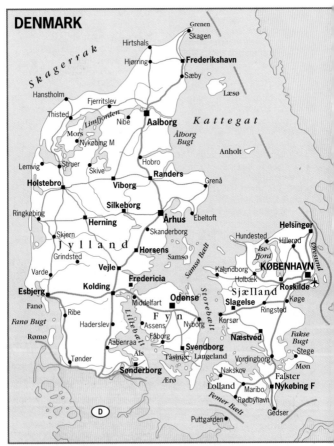

The 18th century was disastrous for Copenhagen: it was badly damaged by two large fires and many people died in a plague. In the 1750s King Frederik V attempted to expand the city and designed some fine houses around Amalienborg. At the end of the century Copenhagen became embroiled in the Napoleonic Wars and the Battle of Copenhagen was fought against the English in 1801. Six years later the English came back, demanding the surrender of the Danish fleet, and bombarded the city.

The industrial revolution of the 19th century brought a sudden boost to the economy as factories and workers' houses were built. The city's ramparts came down in 1867 and were replaced by a string of parks.

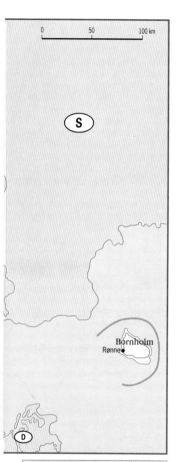

1996 – Europe's Cultural Capital
Copenhagen laid on an ambitious and hugely successful programme of events during 1996, as the 12th Cultural Capital of Europe, with exhibitions, performances and new art commissions. The spirit of 1996 will live on in many new and restored buildings and environmental projects.

WHAT TO SEE

Castles

◆◆
AMALIENBORG
Amalienborg Slotsplads
The residence of the Danish Royal family was built around 1750 as part of Frederik V's grandiose scheme to expand Copenhagen. An equestrian statue of him stands in the octagonal courtyard, surrounded by four rococo palaces. The public may now visit Christian VIII's palace and see the lavishly furnished rooms. At noon each day, the blue-uniformed Royal Life Guards change with complicated manoeuvres, having marched along the streets from Rosenborg Slot, accompanied by a band.

◆◆
CHRISTIANSBORG SLOT (CHRISTIANSBORG PALACE)
Christiansborg Slotsplads
This green-roofed complex was built in the 1920s over Bishop Absalon's original 12th-century castle (whose ruins can be seen below the palace).
The **Royal Reception Rooms** (conducted tours only) are opulent, though unfurnished, richly decorated with Italian chandeliers, silk wall coverings and ornamental plasterwork, and are only used for state occasions. In the same complex are the **Folketing** (parliament – conducted tours only), the **Royal Stables** (in a surviving wing of an 18th-century palace) and the **Theatre Museum** with old costumes, dressing rooms and models of stage sets.

◆◆◆
ROSENBORG SLOT ✓
(ROSENBORG CASTLE)

Østervoldgade 4A
Christian IV created Kongens Have (the King's Garden) in 1606 and within it built Rosenborg. This green-roofed extravaganza of spires and towers, surrounded by a moat and extensive park, was the home of the Danish royal family for nearly a century after its completion in 1633. The brick building, in Dutch Renaissance style, survived bombardments and fires and the exterior is unchanged.

Though exquisitely furnished, it is surprisingly informal, and shows the changing whims and fancies of the Danish monarchy. The rooms are arranged in chronological order: those from the time of Christian IV to Frederik IV have been faithfully preserved, while rooms from later periods have been accurately re-created.

The small rooms are packed with royal treasures – paintings, porcelain, Venetian glass, silver and ivory figures. The decorations include painted ceilings, Flemish tapestries, and an amber chandelier.

The most memorable rooms include the Winter Room with its Antwerp paintings, Frederik III's Marble Room, and Frederik IV's Mirror Cabinet, where the walls, ceiling and the centre of the floor are made of mirror glass. There is even a tiled bathroom, with running water, installed by Christian IV in 1616. The most magnificent room is the Long Hall, with stucco reliefs on the ceiling depicting political events of the time, two thrones guarded by silver lions, tapestries, Dutch fireplaces and silver mirrors. Finally, the tour descends to the basement where the crown jewels are kept – priceless pearls and diamonds, set in crowns, swords and mirrors, as well as an orb and sceptre.

Waterfront of the Nyhavn canal

Churches

HOLMENS KIRKE
Holmens Kanal
With its green copper tower
and Dutch gable ends, this
attractive old church was
transformed from a forge by
Christian IV. It was intended for
the use of sailors – two model
ships hang from the ceiling – a
common feature of Danish
churches. It has a baroque oak
reredos and a carved pulpit.

MARMORKIRKEN (MARBLE
CHURCH)
Frederiksgade 4
This church was to have been
the centre of the new area
around Amalienborg, planned
during the reign of Frederik V,
who laid the foundation stone in
1749. In 1770 the money ran out
(the Norwegian marble was
expensive) and the church was
not completed until 1894.
Statues of famous Danes stand
inside and out.
The dome, one of the biggest in
Europe – 90 feet (30m) in
diameter – is supported on
columns and decorated with
coloured frescoes. You can go
up to the gallery and out to the
edge of the dome to enjoy
far-reaching views.

VOR FRELSERS KIRKE (OUR
SAVIOUR'S CHURCH)
Skt Annæ Gade
Completed in 1696, the interior
of this church, with its gold-
starred vaulted ceiling, contains
several angelic groups and the
carved wooden organ case
rests on two elephants.

The unusual exterior has a pale
turquoise spire, around which
curves a staircase guarded by
railings. At the top stands the
figure of Christ on a globe.

Museums

ARBEJDERMUSEET
(WORKERS' MUSEUM)
Rømersgade 22
This educative and interesting
museum shows Copenhagen's
social changes over the last
century through reconstructions
of three typical workers' homes
and workplaces from the 1870s,
1930s and 1950s.
Old-style streets, backyards
and workshops lead into
cramped houses, furnished in
period styles.
For refreshment, pay a visit to
the simple basement Café
& Øl-Halle 1892 which serves
food and beer from that era, or
the 1930s Civic Restaurant.
Both charge modern prices.
The museum frequently holds
temporary exhibitions.

FRIHEDSMUSEET
(RESISTANCE MUSEUM)
Churchillparken
Outside this museum stands the
German armoured car in which
the Danes brought news of the
Nazi surrender. Inside, the
museum graphically relates
how initial civil resistance to the
German occupation eventually
turned to active sabotage.
Tribute is paid to the British
Royal Air Force who supplied
radio transmitters and to those
who smuggled out Jews. This
museum recently underwent
renovation.

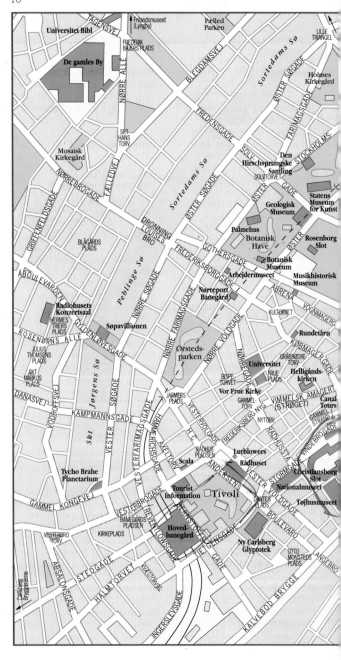

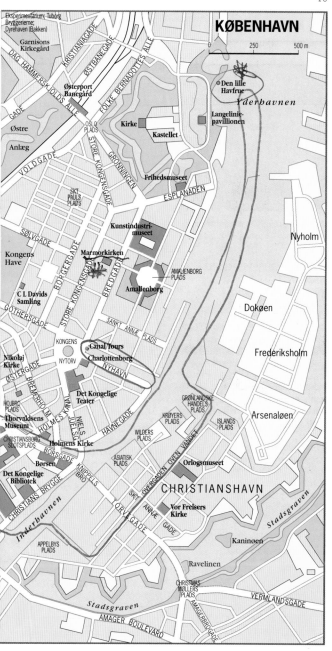

KØBENHAVN

Eksperimentarium; Tuborg
Bryggerierne;
Dyrehaven (Bakken)

Garnisons
Kirkegård

KRISTIANIAGADE

ØSTBANEGADE

DAG HAMMERSKJOLDS ALLE

FOLKE BERNADOTTES ALLE

Østerport
Banegård

OSLO
PLADS

GADE

Østre

Anlæg

VOLDGADE

STORE KONGENSGADE

GRØNNINGEN

Den lille
Havfrue

Yderhavnen

Langelinie-
pavillionen

Kirke

Kastellet

Frihedsmuseet

ESPLANADEN

Nyholm

SKT
PAULS
PLADS

SØLVGADE

Kunstindustri-
museet

Kongens
Have

BORGERGADE

Marmorkirken

BREDGADE

AMALIENBORG
PLADS

C L Davids
Samling

GOTHERSGADE

STORE KONGENSGADE

Amalienborg

Dokøen

SANKT ANNÆ PLADS

Frederiksholm

KONGENS

NYTORV

Canal Tours

Charlottenborg

NYHAVN

Arsenaløen

Nikolaj
Kirke

ØSTERGADE

BREMERHOLM

HOLMENS KANAL

Det Kongelige
Teater

HAVNEGADE

GRØNLANDSKE
HANDELS
PLADS

KRØYERS
PLADS

ISLANDS
PLADS

HØJBRO
PLADS

Thorvaldsens
Museum

CHRISTIANSBORG
SLOTSPLADS

NIELS JUELSGADE

Holmens Kirke

WILDERS
PLADS

Børsen

BORSGADE

ÅSIATISK
PLADS

Det Kongelige
Bibliotek

KNIPPELS
BRO

OVERGADEN OVEN VANDET

Orlogsmuseet

CHRISTIANS BRYGGE

Inderhavnen

SKT ANNÆ GADE

TORVEGADE

CHRISTIANSHAVN

Vor Frelsers
Kirke

Stadsgraven

APPELBYS
PLADS

Kaninøen

Ravelinen

CHRISTMAS
MØLLERS
PLADS

AMAGERBROGADE

VERMLANDSGADE

Stadsgraven

AMAGER BOULEVARD

0   250   500 m

A statue of Denmark's most famous writer: Hans Christian Andersen

◆◆
DEN HIRSCHSPRUNGSKE SAMLING (THE HIRSCHSPRUNG COLLECTION)

Stockholmsgade 20
Patron of the arts Heinrich Hirschsprung (1836–1908), a tobacco manufacturer, gave the nation his private collection of paintings, sculptures, drawings and water colours. The museum is housed in a charming building in a park. The works in the collection are by 19th- and 20th-century Danish artists, some of whose rooms have been re-created here. Paintings by Eckersberg, Købke and Lundbye represent the Golden Age; works by the Skagen and Funen painters are also on display.

Louis Tussaud's Wax Museum
H C Andersens Boulevard 22
Mix with politicians, actors, entertainers and historical figures in the world of wax. A Chamber of Horrors and Fairy-tale Land complete the tour.

NATIONALMUSEET (THE NATIONAL MUSEUM)

Ny Vestergade 10
In this vast museum are some outstanding finds illustrating Denmark's cultural history from the prehistoric to the present day. It is particularly strong on the Bronze Age and the Vikings. The museum is split into five sections. The **Danish Department** goes from prehistoric times up until the mid-19th century while the **Ethnographic Section** has items from non-European peoples (such as the Inuit). The **Department of Egyptian, Greek and Roman Antiquities** has some fine objects and the collection of coins and medals is outstanding. In the **Children's Museum** is a 'time machine', with a tunnel of sound and light. Highlights include a tiny Bronze Age chariot (1400 BC) pulling a golden disc representing the sun, and Danish domestic interiors which show how different strata of society lived from the 17th century onwards. The Victorian Home (Klunkehjem) shows the cosy interior of a family house. A fascinating section on the Middle Ages includes displays of handicrafts, trades (old shoes and gold rings) and church interiors, as well as the Norsemen in Greenland.

◆◆◆
NY CARLSBERG GLYPTOTEK

Dantes Plads 7
This museum houses the private collection of Carl Jacobsen of the Carlsberg brewery family, donated to the public in 1888.

Deep green tranquillity at Ny Carlsberg Glyptotek

One of the most arresting features on the ground floor is a conservatory, with the *Water Mother* by the Danish sculptor, Kai Nielsen, set in a pond and framed by palms and lush greenery. The largest room is the columned Banqueting Hall, in the style of a Greek temple, now used for concerts. It is ringed by sculpture galleries – mainly torsos and marble busts from Greece, Rome and the Near East.

The Egyptian section has painted coffins and delightful bronze animals found in tombs. Work by 19th- and 20th-century Danish sculptors and paintings from the Danish Golden Age are on show. A new extension in a courtyard houses bronzes by Degas and works by Rodin, as well as French Impressionists, Monet, Pissarro and Gauguin.

◆◆◆
ORLOGSMUSEET (ROYAL DANISH NAVAL MUSEUM)
Overgaden oven Vandet 58A
Situated on the picturesque Christianshavn canal in a former naval hospital, the museum tells the story of the Danish Navy. The beautifully arranged exhibits show not only model and lifesize ships (including a 12-oar boat and the Royal Barge), but also portraits, weapons, naval artillery and many objects from shipwrecks.

◆◆◆
STATENS MUSEUM FOR KUNST (ROYAL MUSEUM OF FINE ARTS)
Sølvgade 48–50
In Denmark's National Gallery is a rich collection once owned by Danish kings. The large stately building is divided into two sections: non-Danish artists (including Rubens, Hals and Matisse); while the Danish

section holds the country's national collection of drawings, sculpture and graphic art. One room is devoted to Vilhelm Hammershøi (1864–1916). A new extension has been built and houses 20th-century art and a children's museum.

◆◆
THORVALDSENS MUSEUM
Porthusgade 2
This distinctive polychrome building opened in 1848 to house the works of Copenhagen-born Bertel Thorvaldsen (1770–1844), a prolific sculptor whose fine statues are found in many European cities. He lived in Rome for 40 years, and the exterior frieze depicts his return home and the transport of his sculptures to the museum. Inside is larger-than-life statuary of classical and biblical figures. Thorvaldsen originally modelled in clay which cracks when it dries, so he transformed his still-damp figures into more stable plaster. Over many years however, pollution has discoloured many of the works. The museum also contains Thorvaldsen's library, paintings, coins and bronzes.

◆◆
TØJHUSMUSEET (THE ROYAL DANISH ARSENAL MUSEUM)
Tøjhusgade 3
Officials in red jackets, black tricorn hats and white gloves (a modified version of late 16th-century artillery uniform) greet visitors to this museum which shows the rise and fall of Denmark's military power. It is housed in Europe's longest vaulted Renaissance hall, the Cannon Hall, built around 1600, and includes a fine collection of muskets, gun carriages, cannon balls and many model sailing ships.
From 1648 the museum stored war trophies, and 200 years later it became the repository of the royal arms collection.

◆
TYCHO BRAHE PLANETARIUM
Gammel Kongevej 10
In the Planetarium are 'hands-on' models, films and laser displays to help visitors answer astronomical questions, about exploration of the universe and the mysteries of the cosmos.

The beautiful Tivoli Gardens

Other Sights

◆◆
RUNDETÅRN (ROUND TOWER)

Købmagergade 52

On the initiative of King Christian IV this tower was built as an observatory in 1642, to be part of the new university complex. The King himself wrote the words on the gilded inscription, in rebus form. Around the edge of the viewing platform, nearly 96 feet (29m) above street level, runs a lovely wrought iron lattice.

Its unique feature is the ascent, a spiral ramp of 685 feet (209m) to enable the observatory equipment to be carried up. It is the oldest functioning observatory in Europe and is open to the public in winter. The original church and library were burnt down in 1728 (later rebuilt – the present church is a rococo delight), but the solid tower survived and the climb to the top is worth the effort.

◆◆◆
TIVOLI GARDENS

Centrally situated opposite the railway station, this amusement park-cum-pleasure gardens was opened in 1843 and is still immensely popular. From opening time (11.00hrs, end of April to mid-September only) when families and local pensioners arrive, until early evening when city workers drop by for a waffle, a sausage, or a glass of beer, the gardens continually buzz with activity and shrieks from the thrill rides. At dusk, thousands of coloured lamps lure in tourists for a meal at one of its 30 or so restaurants, (many exotically designed), or entertainment at the concert hall or at one of the theatres.

The successful ingredients are a pleasant setting – trees, lakes and a profusion of flowers – on which has been superimposed a large and irresistible funfair. The Tivoli Guards, musically gifted boys aged 9 to 16, wearing bearskins, red jackets and white trousers (the uniform of the Royal Life Guards), march through the Gardens at weekends and give free weekly concerts. Other free entertainment includes afternoon concerts, events on the open-air stage, evening ballet and mime at the Pantomime Theatre, and afternoon performances at the Children's Theatre. Stars of international repute play at the concert hall and cabaret theatre. Firework displays round off the evening twice a week. In 1993, Tivoli celebrated its 150th birthday and the **Tivoli Museet** opened to mark the occasion. It tells the history of the Gardens, by means of films, models and mementoes.

Tourist Information Office
The Copenhagen Tourist Information Office (tel: 33 11 13 25) is at Bernstorffsgade 1 which is at the junction with Vesterbrogade, on the corner of Tivoli and incorporates an accommodation service (tel: 33 12 28 80). It is very close to the main railway station and not far from the Rådhuspladsen. (See page 119 for opening times.)

COPENHAGEN

Entertainment

Copenhagen is the liveliest city in Scandinavia, not just Denmark, offering a wide choice of evening entertainment. All events are listed in the free monthly English publication *Copenhagen This Week*, available from the Tourist Office, hotels and the airport. Plays (sometimes in English) and ballet are performed at several theatres, and in the open air during the summer, in museum courtyards (at the Kunstindustrimuseet, for example). Concerts are staged at the **Danish Radio Concert Hall**, the **Concert Hall** at **Tivoli** and in churches. The opera and ballet seasons run from September to June on two stages of the **Royal Theatre**. A puppet theatre performs in the open air in **Kongens Have**. Many cinemas show films in the original language with Danish subtitles.

Live Music and Dancing

Copenhagen provides free music on summer weekends in **Amager Strandpark** (Saturday afternoons, rock) and in **Fælledparken** (Sundays). In the evenings, city bars, cafés and clubs, especially around

Clubs

As transient as popular taste, new clubs pop up, old ones disappear. For up-to-date information, ask at the tourist office or your hotel. The booklet *Copenhagen This Week* has a full list. Free disco tickets are often handed out in the streets.

Vestergade, throb with all kinds of music.

Pubs, piano bars and nightclubs attract many tourists, but it is jazz that many visitors go for, as Copenhagen is an important centre for this music. The **Copenhagen Jazz House** at Niels Hemmingsen Gade, (live music Thursday to Sunday), is the top spot for Danish musicians, and international artists during the annual jazz festival. New cafés around Skt Hans Torv in the Norrebrø area, now offer music (rock, punk, fusion and acoustic jazz) as an extra attraction. These include **Ca'feen Funkie** and **Barcelona** (mostly jazz); **Café Rust** and **Bananrepublikken**. **La Fontaine** (Kompagnistræde 11) pulls in late crowds, and Finn Ziegler now plays at **Finn Ziegler's Hjørne**, 24 Vodroffsvej. The best blues centre is **Mojo** found on Longangsstræde, northeast of Tivoli, while the noisiest **rock** blasts out from the nearby **Drop Inn**.

If you're lured into a **nightclub** by a pretty girl, watch the prices. Unsuspecting tourists have paid hundreds of kroner for a bottle of beer and the promise of a striptease.

Discos

Most start around midnight and carry on until 05.00 or 06.00hrs. The atmosphere is casual and drink prices are reasonable. **Woodstock** at Vestergade 12 plays soul, rock and 60s music, or try **Annabels** (Lille Kongensgade 16), and two in Gothersgade – the **Duke** (at 13) and **X-Ray** (at 8).

Accommodation

Most visitors to Copenhagen come on a package tour, being allocated, or selecting from, a handful of hotels chosen by the tour operator. There is often a considerable price difference between rooms with and without private bathrooms. Independent travellers who don't want to spend too much could consider one of the following hotels which are all quite central; most only serve breakfast. The **Absalon** (tel: 31 24 22 11) in Helgolandsgade, behind the station, has nearly 500 beds and has recently been refurbished; it offers baby-sitting services. Two hotels very close to Rådhuspladsen, each with just over 100 beds, are **Hotel Alexandra** (tel: 33 14 22 00) with its own restaurant, and **Ascot Hotel** (tel: 33 12 60 00) with its own garage. A fairly new hotel is **Cab Inn** (tel: 31 21 04 00) in Danasvej (about five minutes by bus from Vesterport Station or by rail from Central Station). Bedrooms resemble a ship's cabin and are somewhat cramped, but they are clean

One of the many restaurants found in Tivoli Gardens

and cheap. A cafeteria service provides breakfast. For a family atmosphere, you could try **Ibsens Hotel** (tel: 33 13 19 13), run by three ladies, in the Frederiksborg district (northwest) of Copenhagen, 10 minutes' bus ride from the centre; it has a garage.
The accommodation service at the tourist office can, for a small fee, arrange hotel, or private accommodation. However, in peak season it is advisable to book in advance, either direct with the hotel, or: Hotelbooking København, Bernstorffsgade 1, DK-1577, Copenhagen V (tel: 33 12 28 80).

Restaurants

With over 2,000 eating places in Copenhagen, visitors are spoilt for choice. By law, restaurants must display their prices, and there are no extras – tips are included in the bills. All the city's restaurants – American to vegetarian – are listed in *Copenhagen This Week*.

The Lurblowers statue

Transport

Copenhagen runs an integrated transport system, so that the same ticket (sold by bus drivers and at station booking offices), can be used on buses and S-trains (see page 121). The city is split into zones and one basic ticket entitles you to one hour's travel, including transfers, within the zone you start from, and to adjacent zones. You pay extra for travel to other zones. If you are planning several journeys, it is cheaper to buy a *10-turistklippekort* (Clip Card) valid for ten rides within two or three zones. Each time you start a ride, you must stamp your ticket (face up) at the machine found by the driver on buses, or in the yellow machine on station platforms, before boarding trains.

For lunch, try a *smørrebrød*. **Ida Davidsen** (St Kongensgade 70) and **Kanal-Kafeen** (Frederiksholms Kanal 18) specialise in them. Cellar restaurants such as **Thorvaldsen** (34 Gammel Strand) and **Café Charlottenborg** (Nyhavn 2) provide a good lunch and a pleasant ambience. A substantial two-course meal (*dagens ret*) can be bought in department stores such as **Illum**. For dinner, two good quality, if expensive, fish restaurants are **Krogs Fiskerestaurant** (38 Gammel Strand) and **Den Gyldne Fortun** (Ved Stranden 18). Don't ignore the main railway station with its bars and restaurants, including the **Bistro** and **Grillen**, which specialise in Swedish salmon and roast beef. Slightly cheaper are **Sporvejen** (Gråbrødretorv 17) and **Galathea Kroen** (Rådhusstræde 9).

Copenhagen Card

Purhase of this card, for one, two or three days, entitles you to free travel on buses and S-trains within Copenhagen, and also on mainline trains and long-distance buses within the whole of North Zealand, which includes Roskilde and Køge. It also gives you free admission to over 60 attractions and museums, (including the Louisiana Museum and Tivoli), a 20 per cent discount on Canal and City Tours, and 25 to 50 per cent discount on crossings to Sweden. An information booklet about the museums is included. If you are planning to do a lot of sightseeing, this card is excellent value.

Excursions from Copenhagen

Dyrehaven (Deer Park), once a royal hunting ground, is a large wooded and parkland area on the coast 6 miles (10km) north of Copenhagen, where herds of deer still roam.

In one corner is **Bakken**, a 400-year old amusement park, open end-March to end-August. It is older than Tivoli (and free), with over 100 fairground attractions. South of the city, on the dunes of Strandparken, stands the new **Museum of Modern Art**, a huge ship-like building in white concrete with 10,000 square yards (8,360sq m) space; ideal for exhibiting large items of sculpture. The Museum opened in 1996 with an Emil Nolde exhibition.

Two attractive beaches north of town are **Charlottenlund Fort** and **Bellevue**.

On Mondays...

Monday is not the best day for sightseeing as some of the most important art museums are closed. Be sure to check with *Copenhagen This Week* before you set off.

Copenhagen's bustling Town Hall Square

EXCURSIONS FROM COPENHAGEN

◆◆
BRYGGERIERNE (BREWERIES)
Hellerup

Denmark's two largest breweries, Carlsberg and Tuborg, are now part of one company and each runs very popular free guided tours round their plants, which end with free samples.

The processes are highly automated, from steeping barley to bottling the beer and visitors are taken from one part of the plant to another by bus. At Tuborg they are shown the 85-foot (26m) bottle built for an industrial exhibition in 1888 which holds the equivalent of 1.5 million ordinary bottles.

◆◆
EKSPERIMENTARIUM
Hellerup

This science centre near the Tuborg Brewery is popular particularly with children. It aims to promote interest in science and technology, and has set up a range of interesting hands-on experiments – testing your lungs, playing with light and ozone shadows, for example – within the context of studying man, nature and their interaction.

◆◆
FRILANDSMUSEET
Lyngby

Frilandsmuseet is an open-air museum set in the peaceful wooded countryside at Lyngby, some 8 miles (13km) north of Copenhagen.

Nearly 100 old Danish farms and cottages from the 17th to the 19th centuries have been dismantled, moved and reassembled here. All the buildings have been authentically furnished in different regional styles and are surrounded by flocks of sheep and geese. Threshing and weaving demonstrations re-create old-style rural life.

> **Watch Out for Cyclists**
> Before stepping off a bus in any Danish city, look carefully to the right, as there is a cycle track between the road and the pavement along which bikers glide almost soundlessly.

A tall ship on Copenhagen's Nyhavn canal is a reminder of the graceful days of sail

FUNEN (FYN)

The smallest of Denmark's three main islands, Funen is the prettiest, particularly in the south where there are rolling hills and an attractive archipelago. Apart from an industrial area north of Odense, the island is mainly agricultural, growing most of Denmark's fruit and vegetables. The countryside is dotted with grand manor houses and thatched cottages. The shallow sea is safe for children, and many beaches have received the EU Blue Flag award.

Getting There

Road bridges link Funen (Middlefart) to Jutland (E20) and to Langeland and Tasinge. Frequent ferry services ply from Korsør (Zealand) to Nyborg and from Gelting (northern Germany) to Faborg.

Good Connections

Denmark is undertaking two bridge building projects between its own islands and Sweden. Both links consist of two bridges, artificial islands and a tunnel, and will carry traffic and trains. The 11-mile-(18km) long **Great Belt fixed link** will connect Knudshoved in Funen with Halsskov in Zealand: its 4-mile (6.8km) East Bridge is the world's largest offshore suspension bridge and will carry a four-lane motorway. The **Halsskov Exhibition Centre** shows how the work is progressing. The 10-mile-(16km) long **Øresund fixed link** will link Kastrup (Copenhagen's airport) to Lernacken, located southwest of Malmo.

The eccentric Egeskov Castle

WHAT TO SEE

♦♦♦
EGESKOV ✓

This private home is a romantic, turretted castle, which claims to be the best-kept Renaissance island castle in Europe. Its most attractive moated setting is matched by its beautiful interior, perhaps somewhat contrived as the rooms have been specially arranged to fit a theme or period, rather than being left as they were.

The castle, finished in 1554, was built on a foundation of oak piles driven in to the lake – Egeskov means oak forest – and apparently a whole forest was used. The thick walls hide secret staircases, a well and chimneys. The **Jagstuen** (Hunting Room) and the **Jagtgangen** (Hunting Corridor) may not appeal to animal lovers – they are hung with trophies, including a lion, a cheetah and elephant tusks, killed by a former owner, Count Gregers Ahlefeldt– Laurvig–Bille. The huge, beamed **Riddersalen** (Knights' Hall) is empty except

for its large paintings, but is often used for concerts. The castle contains much fine furniture and art. In the large grounds there are sparkling fountains, several children's play areas and a Japanese tower hides in the bamboo **maze**. Four barns in the grounds now house museums: the **Veteranmuseum** contains old cars and aircraft; the **Motorcycle Museum** is home to renovated motor bikes; the **Hestevogns og Landsbrugs Museum** (Horse and Carriage and Agricultural Museum) shows old farm tools and the **Museum of Peculiarities** displays old TV sets and push-bikes.
Egeskov is at Kværndrup 15½ miles (25km) southeast of Odense.

Fåborg's carillon plays hymns daily

◆◆◆
FÅBORG

The centre of this little town is delightful, like a living museum, with photo-opportunities galore amongst its cobbled streets lined with picturesque buildings. It is situated on the southwest coast of Funen and at various times belonged to Denmark and Schleswig. In the 18th century it owned one of the largest fleets in Denmark and was an important trading town. Today, boats ply to Gelting (Germany) and to nearby Danish islands (Ærø, Lyø and Avernakø).

Sightseeing

Den Gamle Gård (The Old Merchant's House) was built in 1725, and once belonged to Mr Voigt, whose daughter was an early love of Hans Christian Andersen. Now it re-creates life around 1800 in a series of rooms, from the kitchen, with its boxbed for the maid and hatch for the brooding goose, to the grander master's bedroom. Other rooms display glass, china, textiles and local gravestones.
Fåborg Museum for Fynsk Malerkunst (of Funen Painting) exhibits mainly local landscapes by the best-known Funen painters, including Peter Hansen, Johannes Larsen and Fritz Syberg from 1880 to 1920. There are also portraits, still lifes and seascapes, as well as powerful paintings by Kristian Zahrtmann, who strongly influenced the Funen group. They selected and sold their paintings to wine-factory owner Mads Rasmussen, who helped establish this museum.

The **Klokketårnet** (clock tower) is Fåborg's landmark, and has Funen's largest carillon. Its church is long since gone but two others remain: **Horne Kirke**, a 12th-century round church with a crucifix from the Middle Ages and a font which was made by Thorvaldsen; **Helligåndskirken** (Church of the Holy Ghost), built as part of a monastery – King Christian's Bible lies on the altar.

Excursions from Fåborg

At **Grubbe**, to the west, are an old Dutch windmill and a watermill, both in working order, and at **Kaleko** (northeast) is the country's oldest watermill, furnished to show a miller's lifestyle.

Accommodation

In town, **Hotel Strandgade** (tel: 62 61 20 12) offers comfortable accommodation while the half-timbered **Youth Hostel** at Grønnegade 71–2 is one of the most popular in Denmark (tel: 62 61 12 03).

The modern **Interscan Hotel Faaborg Fjord** (tel: 62 61 10 10), a mile (2km) southeast of the town by the harbour, is elegantly furnished and stands in its own grounds.

Two places near Fåborg are full of character. **Steensgård Herregårdspension** (tel: 62 61 94 90) at Millinge, northwest of Fåborg, is a grand moated manor house set in a park. In contrast, **Faldsled Kro**, in the pretty village of Faldsled, is a group of thatched buildings by the sea, with an attractive garden (tel: 62 68 11 11). Both hotels serve excellent meals.

Restaurants

The atmospheric **Mouritz**, on Østergade, the main street, is open daily for long hours, while **Ved Brønden**, in the square, specialises in fish dishes.

NYBORG

Nyborg is an old harbour town on the east of Funen, on the historic trading route between Jutland and Zealand – a role which will continue when the new Storebælt (Great Belt) bridges and tunnel linking Funen to Zealand are completed. The 4-mile (6.6km) West Bridge is the longest combined road and railway bridge in Europe (see page 29).

In medieval times, Nyborg was the capital of Denmark, and it has succeeded in preserving some of its past in spite of damage inflicted during the wars against Sweden and by occupying Spanish troops in the Napoleonic Wars.

More recently, several rather intrusive modern buildings have been constructed amongst the old houses and cobbled streets.

Sightseeing

The oldest surviving building is **Nyborg Slot** (Nyborg Castle), founded in 1170 as part of a chain of coastal forts to fend off Denmark's enemies. In the Middle Ages, Danish kings lived and held court here. The castle is partly surrounded by water, and in the restored wing (Knudstårn) there are fortress remains and a collection of various weapons

The **Landporten** (Town Gate)

which dates from 1660 is the oldest in Denmark and forms part of the original ramparts. Another fine old medieval building is the **Mads Lerches Gård**, now the Nyborg Regional Museum. In the two-storey, half-timbered house, the rooms have been laid out so as to show the lifestyle of a rich merchant.

The **Vor Frue Kirke** (Church of Our Lady) was founded in 1388.

Close by is the **Korsbrødre-gården**, once part of a monastery, whose Gothic arched cellar is now a shop.

Accommodation and Restaurants

Hesselhuset (tel: 65 31 24 48) is a restaurant which benefits from good views across the Great Belt, and **Hotel Nyborg Strand** (tel: 65 31 31 31) is a large hotel in its own grounds.

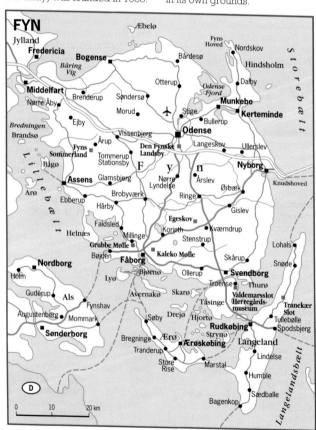

◆◆◆
ODENSE ✓

Odense, Funen's main town and Denmark's third largest, is famous as the birthplace of the writer of fairytales, Hans Christian Andersen. It derives its name from the Norse god, Odin. In the Middle Ages the town attracted pilgrims to Skt Albani Kirke (St Alban's Church) where King Knud (Canute) was murdered and later canonised. Odense has always been an important trading town, and when a canal was dug to Kerteminde, the town's commercial future was assured.

Today, the city is sliced in two by the ring road (O1), and is dominated by the huge skyscraper block of Sparekassen Bikuben Fyn. Exploring the town on foot, it becomes apparent that today's citizens are desperately trying to make amends for the destruction they and their forebears wrought, by carefully restoring the surviving old buildings and creating some superb museums.

The city is well endowed with parks, there is a lovely riverside walk along the Odense Å and also river cruises (see page 36).

Sightseeing

Brandts Klædefabrik, Brandts Passage 37–43, once a cloth mill and Odense's largest workplace, has been cleverly renovated to become Denmark's first international art and cultural centre. Contained in the four-storey building (no lift) are the **Kunsthallen** (art gallery) with changing exhibitions, three museums, and live entertainment in the Amphitheater (courtyard).

The **Museet for Fotokunst** (Museum of Photographic Art) has a permanent photo collection and temporary exhibitions.

The **Danmarks Grafiske Museum** (Danish Museum of Printing) displays a range of old printing machines showing the development of the industry over the last 300 years. Every morning retired workers demonstrate their skills in lithography, bookbinding and other processes. The **Dansk Pressemuseum** (Danish Press Museum) catalogues the history of the Danish press from 1666. As well as a rotary printing press, the museum shows yellowed newspapers, many showing evidence of the censors, and an editor's office dating from around 1900.

In an adjacent building, the **Tidens Samling** (Time Collection) has tableaux of domestic design and fashion in this century.

The **Carl Nielsen Museet** is appropriately situated adjoining the Odense Concert Hall, Claus Bergs Gade 11, and traces the life (1865–1931) of Denmark's most famous composer of operas, symphonies and popular songs. Born near Odense, he married the gifted sculptress Anne Marie Brodersen, whose work is also displayed. As well as mementoes of their European travels, programmes and scores of Nielsen's works, his medals, and reports of his state-like funeral, there are re-creations of their cluttered rooms – her studio, his music room – all viewed to the accompaniment of the composer's own music. Headphones are available and there is a video show.

The **Fyns Kustmuseum** (Funen Art Gallery), Jernbanegade 13, in a classical building erected less than a century ago, exhibits pictures by Danish artists from Jens Juel to Asger Jorn, including the Funen painters, active at the turn of the century. A section displays sculpture along with Constructivist art.

The two museums devoted to Hans Christian Andersen may come as a disappointment, particularly to children. The **Hans Christian Andersens Barndomshjem** (Childhood Home), Munkemøllestræde 3–5, where the writer lived from 1807 to 1819, is a small, unfurnished two-roomed cottage which is now dwarfed by modern buildings.

Instead of items asssociated with Andersen's childhood, it contains early photos and plans of the house and the surrounding area, one letter written by him and a wood engraving.

The much larger museum, **Hans Christian Andersens Hus**, Hans Jensens Stræde 37–45, is in a heavily restored area of cobbled streets and pretty cottages. Andersen was born here in 1805, and the cottage has been extended to accommodate the books and other materials pertaining to his life.

The exhibition demands a lot of reading – of his poems, travel notes and early manuscripts.

Illustrations of his tales are displayed, as are some of his paper cut-outs.

A reconstruction of his room shows old furniture, pictures and personal possessions including a hatbox, suitcase and boots. In a circular memorial hall the walls are decorated with scenes from his life, and in the library are volumes of his works in many different languages. A slide show, along with commentary, narrates his life story and headphones enable visitors to listen to some of his best-known tales.

The **Jernbanemuseet** (Railway Museum) adjoining Odense station is a very popular attraction, with its luxurious royal carriages and a turn-of-the-century station. The museum illustrates the history of the Danish railway from 1847 with actual locomotives and a big model railway track.

The **Møntergården-Odense Bymuseum** (City Museum), Overgade 48–50, attractively displays the town's 1,000-year cultural and urban history in a collection of 16th- and 17th-century buildings.

As well as re-creating medieval Odense through finds and photographs from excavations, the museum presents older reconstructed buildings, including St Alban's wooden church, and a Dominican abbey with realistic tableaux of monks at work. The coin and medal collection is said to be the finest in the country. In addition to this there is an interesting toy exhibition, and a display of women's clothing and embroidered samplers.

Skt Knuds Domkirke

Skt Knuds Domkirke (St Canute's Cathedral), Flakhaven, is a lofty Gothic edifice dating from about 1300. The finely carved gold and black altarpiece, by the 16th-century Lübeck craftsman Claus Berg, together with the stained glass window, adds colour to the white interior. In the crypt are the remains of King Canute, killed in St Albans Church; the contents of a second coffin are disputed – either Canute's brother Benedict or St Alban himself, brought back to Denmark by Canute. Hans Christian Anderson was confirmed here.

Skt Hans Kirke, Nørregade, was started a bit later as an abbey church and is the only Danish church with an exterior pulpit. The vaulted interior has a carved pulpit and frescoes.

Accommodation

Odense is not only popular because of Hans Andersen, but also as a conference centre. Hotel standards are high, as are the prices. Two cheaper hotels are the centrally located **Ydes Hotel** (tel: 66 12 11 31), an old building, recently extended, and **Hotel Domir** (tel: 66 12 12 47). The central **Det Lille Hotel** (tel: 66 12 28 21) has 14 rooms. Another option is to stay outside Odense. **Mørkenborg Kro og Motel** (tel: 64 83 10 51), founded in 1771, is at Veflinge, 11 miles (18km) northwest of Odense, in lovely surroundings. **Bogense Hotel** (tel: 64 81 11 08) in Bogense, a coastal market town about 18½ miles (30km) from Odense, is comfortable and serves good food.

Restaurants

Restaurants proliferate, not only along the streets, but also in museums, and in the shopping complex at Rosengårdcentret. One of the prettiest is **Under Lindetræt**, in a half-timbered house near Hans Christian Andersen's Museum. It serves *nouvelle cuisine* (tel: 66 12 92 86).

Den Gamle Kro (Overgade 23) is also central, with a courtyard (tel: 66 12 14 33).

Entertainment

Serious-minded visitors can hear the Odense Symphony Orchestra in the new **Concert Hall** and even outside it on Saturdays, from the vegetable market. The **Odense Theatre** (plays are performed in Danish only) is the largest.

Jazz lovers can enjoy the 'Summer in Odense' programme. *Sommerjazz med Fyn og Klem* is a two-day jazz festival in June. Other vibrant light entertainment includes: jazz pubs, nightclubs, bars, discos and a casino at the Radisson/SAS **HC Andersen Hotel**. Upmarket jazz is played at the **Cotton Club**, found at Pantheonsgåde 5C.

The **Atlantic Merry Go Round** (Overgåde 45–7) has a disco.

Excursions from Odense

Boats cruise from Munke Mose Park along willow-tree lined banks to Fruens Bøge, from where you can walk to Funen Village (see below), or you can choose to disembark earlier at Tivoli or the zoo.

Further afield, a 16th-century manor house and its more recent outbuildings, is now a cultural centre (**Kulturcenter Hollufgård**), standing in extensive woodlands and meadows southeast of Odense. One of the most important of these outbuildings is the **Fyns Oldtid-Hollufgård** (Funen Prehistory Museum) which displays local archaeological finds in an exciting way. On the first floor is a vast collection of early finds from Funen – stone tools, buckles, spearheads and pots – particularly exciting for local amateur archaeologists who are allowed to handle the pieces.

Outside, a prehistoric trail and landscape have been created, with thatched houses from Viking and Bronze Age times; examples from the Stone and Iron Ages are to follow soon. Sculptures are displayed in the park and there is a sculpture workshop. There are also two golf courses and nature trails.

Den Fynske Landsby (Funen Village) is an attractive open-air museum where over 20 thatched buildings from rural Funen (dating mostly from the 18th and 19th centuries) have been relocated to form a village, complete with homes, a school, a smithy and an almshouse, all furnished in period style. Old farming and cattle-raising methods are employed. In summer, potters and other craftspeople demonstrate their skills. For three weeks each summer a troupe of local children perform musical adaptations of Hans Christian Andersen's fairy tales on the open-air stage.

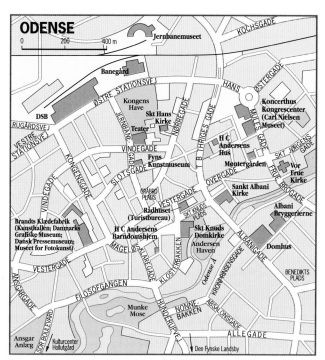

ODENSE

0   200   400 m

Jernbanemuseet

KOCHSGADE

Banegård

ØSTRE STATIONSVEJ

Kongens
Have

Skt Hans
Kirke

HANS

ØSTERGADE

MULES GADE

Koncerthus
Kongrescenter
(Carl Nielsen
Museet)

DSB

RUGÅRDSVEJ

JERNBANE GADE

NØRREGADE

B THIGES GADE

Teater

VINDEGADE

Fyns
Kunstmuseum

SLOTSGADE

H C
Andersens
Hus

SKT JØRGENS GADE

Møntergården

Vor
Frue
Kirke

FRUE BROGADE

Sankt Albani
Kirke

OVERGADE

VESTRE STATIONSVEJ

KONGENSGADE

VINDEGADE

GRÅBRØ
PLADS

VESTERGADE

SKT KNUDS
PLADS

Albani
Bryggerierne

Brandts Klædefabrik
(Kunsthallen; Danmarks
Grafiske Museum;
Dansk Pressemuseum;
Museet for Fotokunst)

Rådhuset
(Turistbureau)

H C Andersens
Barndomshjem

MAGELØS

SKT KNUDS
Domkirke

Andersen
Haven

Domhus

ALBANIGADE

VESTERGADE

KLAREGADE

KLOSTERBAKKEN

Odense Å

KRONPRINSENSGADE

BENEDIKTS
PLADS

ANSGARGADE

FILOSOFGANGEN

Munke
Mose

HUNDERUPVEJ

NONNE-
BAKKEN

ABSALONSGADE

ALLEGADE

Ansgar
Anlæg

SDR BOULEVARD

Kulturcenter
Hollufgård

Den Fynske Landsby

Transport

Local buses are red; long-distance ones are red or yellow. Get on at the back; alight at the front. Different sorts of tickets are available. If your journey entails two or more buses, and will take less than an hour, ask for an *omstigning* (transfer ticket).

◆◆
SVENDBORG

Superbly situated on the Sound at the southeast corner of Funen, Svendborg is the natural gateway to the island of Tåsinge and to the pretty South Funen archipelago; it also makes a good base from which to explore inland Funen.

Odense Fairytale Card

A one- or two-day *eventyr pas* (Fairytale Card) can be bought from the Odense Tourist Bureau, museums and the railway station. It gives free entry to 13 museums (including most listed above), to swimming pools and Funen Village. Reductions are offered on river cruises, and on admission to the Zoo. The pass also provides free local travel on buses and trains.

Yachtsmen come here in large numbers every summer and Svendborg is the starting place for *Fyn rundt*, the annual wooden ships race around the island. Scenically, Svendborg is dominated by its busy harbour: Funen's agricultural products are exported from here and the shipyard is the biggest employer. One of the town's largest factories produces cornflakes for Scandinavia.

Sightseeing
The winding streets go down quite steeply to the harbour, passing between many old half-timbered houses. The grandest is **Anne Hvide's Gård** which dates from about 1560, prominently standing near the main square. Now part of the **Svendborg-og Omegns Museum** (Svendborg County Museum), the rooms are furnished in the styles of the early 18th and early 19th centuries, with portraits and collections of clocks and stoves. Another part of the museum is housed in **Viebæltegård**, the town's former poorhouse, and includes craft workshops (coir mats are still made), local archaeological finds and an apartment from the 1950s. The **Zoologiske Museum** (Zoological Museum) shows the range of Danish animals since the Ice Age, as well as a more recent skeleton – that of a whale, beached locally. Although Svendborg can trace its history back 700 years, and still retains its mill pond, only

Colourful barns relocated at Den Fynske Landsby open-air museum

one church preserves any ancient remains – **Skt Nikolai**, built of large, medieval bricks, with a 16th-century tower and a Skovgaard-painted altar. **Vor Frue Kirke** was orignally Romanesque, but was later rebuilt in Gothic style. It is the prettier and more homely of the two, with a Dutch carillon.

Accommodation
Hotel Christiansminde (tel: 62 21 90 00) is a holiday centre (self-catering as well as a hotel), near woods and beaches and ideal for families. **Hotel Ærø** (tel: 62 21 07 60) is a smaller hotel by the harbour. More costly but central is **Hotel Svendborg** (tel: 62 21 17 00).

Restaurants
All the hotels mentioned above have good restaurants, but you could also try **den Grimme Ælling** (tel: 62 22 21 57) which serves generous buffet lunches, or **Restaurants-Skibet** *Oranje*, a boat moored at Jessens Mole, serving gourmet food.

Entertainment
Several places have live music, including **Børsen Restaurant** once a week. **Under Uret** is a popular pavement café-pub, full of old clocks.

Excursions from Svendborg
The veteran ship *Helge*, built in 1924, sails via the island of Thurø to Valdemars Slot on Tåsinge (see page 41), five times a day in summer – an hour's journey. Other ferries go to the nearby tiny islands of Drejø, Skaro, and Hjortø, and to the larger island of Ærø (see **Funen's Islands**, overleaf).

FUNEN'S ISLANDS

The area around Svendborg is ideal for sailors, with many well-equipped marinas on the islands. The terrain is ideal for cycling – the only means of getting around some places as public transport is limited.

◆
DREJØ

This island of 1,018 acres (412ha), has few trees after a fire 50 years ago. But it has a 16th-century church, a grocer's shop, a restaurant and some overnight accommodation.

◆◆
SKARØ

This is mainly a bird reserve, with salt meadows and fields which are triangular as a result of the enclosure movement. There is one village, and a grill-bar but no restaurant.

◆◆
HJORTØ

This is the smallest of the islands, with wonderful birdlife. Cars and motorbikes are not allowed, and if you want to spend the night here, you will need to bring a tent.

◆◆
LANGELAND

An elongated, mostly flat, cultivated island, Langeland has excellent child-friendly sandy beaches, backed by grass-covered dunes, particularly the northern tip, on the eastern coast and at Ristinge in the southwest.

The island is popular with holiday-makers and has two holiday centres as well as hotels, campsites and lots of summer cottages. Many of the private gardens are beautifully maintained – a local tradition. Evidence of early settlement is seen in the many prehistoric burial mounds including a well-preserved passage grave near Søgård.

Langeland has good ferry links to other islands: to Strynø and Ærø (from Rudkøbing); to Zealand (from Lohals); to Lolland (from Spodsbjerg); to Kiel in Germany (from Bagenkop); and a bridge to Tåsinge.

Sightseeing

◆◆
RUDKØBING

Rudkøbing is the main town on Langeland and is thought to be over 700 years old. Its timber-framed houses, 18th-century buildings and winding streets contribute to its charm. The port is a hive of activity, but while the new yachting marina flourishes, the commercial harbour declines. However fish is still sold on the quayside. The collection housed in the **Langelands Museum** includes numerous prehistoric finds, from the Stone Age onwards. A prized possession is a 2,000-year-old bronze receptacle as well as very early fishing equipment. In **Det gamle Apotek** (the old pharmacy) is a rare collection of chemists' equipment and examples of old-fashioned cures. Another part of the museum (at Østergade 25) concentrates on fishing and sailing. The pretty red-brick, step-gabled 12th-century **church** has gated pews with painted biblical texts. Sightseeing on the rest of the

A fine stretch of open country

island is limited to **Tranekær**, where the **Slotsmølle** (Castle Mill) still produces flour. The moated red-coloured castle, set on a mound, was reconstructed in the last century but is not open; the surrounding park, with rare trees and sculpture is. The adjacent **Slotsmuseum** features local history. Tranekær village, with its half-timbered houses, is most attractive.

Accommodation and Restaurants
Tranekær Gæstgivergård (tel: 62 59 12 04), near the castle is very comfortable and serves meals, as does **Café Herskabs-stalden**, in converted stables. In Rudkøbing, **Hotel Rudkøbing Skudehavn** (tel: 62 51 46 00) is in a lovely position by the harbour.

THURØ
A pretty little rural island, accessible from Svendborg by a causeway. Apart from a 17th-century church, there is little to do but enjoy the countryside and the beaches – Smørmosen has a Blue Flag award.
You can find bed and breakfast places or stay at campsites.

◆◆◆
TÅSINGE
Connected by bridges to both Funen and Langeland, it is easy to drive over Tåsinge without stopping – but that would be a shame. It's a pretty island, hilly in the north, quite flat in the south, but intensely cultivated and dotted with thatched houses and clumps of trees.

Sightseeing
In the little coastal village of **Troense**, which has streets of half-timbered houses, is an outstanding castle and a maritime museum.
The castle **Valdemars Slot** which overlooks a lake, now houses the **Herregårdsmuseum** (locally called the Funen Manor House Museum). It was built in late baroque style by Christian IV for his son, Valdemar. In 1678 the estate was bought and extended by Niels Juel, a naval hero. The grand, spacious rooms have gilded plasterwork, and include a banqueting hall, library and chapel. Tapestries and a fine art collection cover the walls, and much of the beautiful furniture is French.

The **Maritime Collection**, a branch of the Svendborg Museum, is housed in the old village school. The exhibition explains the importance of the sailing ship era; there are also paintings, model ships, wooden figureheads and sailors' souvenirs. West of Troense, **Bregninge** church tower offers a good view.

Accommodation and Restaurants

Hotel Troense (tel: 62 22 54 12) is in the village overlooking the sea, and thatched **Det Lille Hotel** (tel: 62 22 53 41) is more rural. Eat at two old inns – **Bregninge Kro** (tel: 62 22 54 76) near the church, and in Troense, at **Lodskroen Restaurant**.

Aerial view of Æerøskøbing

◆◆◆
ÆRØ ✓

The Danes call this island 'the green pearl' in the south Funen archipelago – the jewel in the crown might be more apt. Ærø is a delightful island, with an undulating landscape dotted with charming villages, windmills and churches. Bird life is abundant along the seashore. Much of the west coast is backed by cliffs, but the east is indented with bays and coves and provides the best beaches. These are Vester at Ærøskøbing, Jørbæk at Søby and Erikshale, near Marstal, which has a Blue Flag. Several ferries sail to Ærø's three harbours: to Marstal from Rudkøbing (on Langeland); to Ærøskøbing from Svendborg

and to Søby from Fåborg (both on Funen). A service runs to Søby from Mommark (on Als island) during the summer. The prettiest route to take is from Svendborg passing many small islands.

Sightseeing
Ærøskøbing is the wonder of Ærø with its perfectly preserved urban layout and its colour-washed timber-framed houses – some leaning dangerously – dating from the 17th and 18th centuries. They cover an extensive area, and visitors strolling through the cobbled streets feel they have stepped back in time. Denmark's oldest post office, dating from 1749, is still in business.

The island's museums give the curious visitor a chance to enter the old, low-ceilinged, tiny-windowed houses. **Ærø Museum**, in the former bailiff's house tells the history of the island from prehistoric times. Displays include textiles, domestic articles, a maritime collection and the interior of an old apothecary's shop. An unusual museum is the **Flaskeskibs-samlingen** (Bottle Ship Collection), also called 'Bottle Peter', where hundreds of old model ships in bottles are displayed together with newer ones made by the late owner, sea captain Peter Jacobsen. In the same building are the Hans Billedhuggers Mindestuer (memorial rooms), displaying examples of his folk art and carvings.
The **Hammerichs Hus** is an 18th-century merchant's house

with locally made glass, furniture, tiles and china. Attractive villages worth visiting on Ærø include **Ommel**, with a tiny harbour and thatched cottages, and **Store Rise**, the location of Ærø's oldest church founded in the 12th century, with a medieval monastery gate. **Bregninge** village in the northwest has a long main street and a very beautiful 13th-century church. Inside are frescoes, and a triptych carved by Claus Berg.
On the coast, the **Voderup Klint** (cliffs), west of Tranderup, provide unusual scenery of large slopes; a footpath leads to the beach.
Marstal, an old maritime town, is now the largest settlement on Ærø. The granite jetty dates from the last century, and wooden boats are still made in the shipyard. The town has a few cobbled streets but a large number of new houses impinge on the old. The **Marstal Søfartsmuseum** (Maritime Museum) shows many models of ships, navigation equipment and sailors' souvenirs.

Accommodation
Two pleasant family hotels in the old part of Ærøskøbing, each with a garden, are **Hotel Ærøhus** (tel: 62 52 10 03) and **Det Lille Hotel** (tel: 62 52 23 00). **Bregninge Kro** is an old inn found en route to Søby (tel: 62 58 18 14).

Restaurants
The hotels listed above have good dining rooms. Another place to try is **Vindeballe Kro** (tel: 62 52 16 13), a charming old country inn in Ærøskøbing.

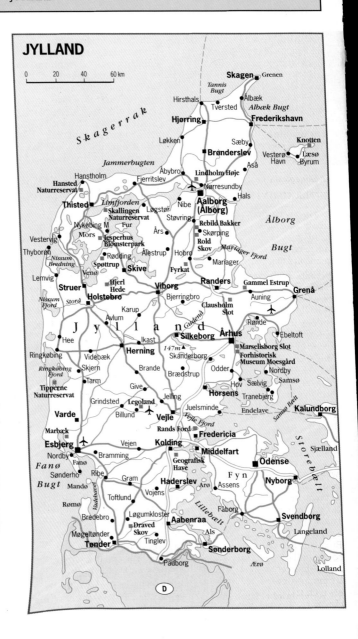

JYLLAND

0   20   40   60 km

Skagen — Grenen
Tannis Bugt
Hirsthals   Ålbæk
Tversted   Albæk Bugt
Hjørring   Frederikshavn

Skagerrak

Løkken   Sæby   Knotten
Brønderslev   Vesterø Læsø
Jammerbugten   Havn Byrum
Åbybro Lindholm Høje   Åså
Hansted   Fjerritslev
Hanstholm   Nørresundby
Hansted   Hals
Naturreservat   Aalborg
Thisted   Limfjorden   (Ålborg)   Ålborg
Skallingen   Nibe
Nykøbing M   Naturreservat   Løgstør Støvring   Rebild Bakker   Bugt
Mors Fur   Års   Skørping
Vesterø Jesperhus   Rold
Thyborøn Blomsterpark   Ålestrup Hobro Skov Mariager Fjord
Nissum   Rødding   Mariager
Bredning Spøttrup Venø Skive Fyrkat
Lemvig   Hjerl   Randers   Gammel Estrup
Struer   Hede   Viborg   Grenå
Nissum   Storå Holstebro   Bjerringbro   Auning
Fjord   Clausholm
Karup   Slot
Avlum   Rønde
Jylland   Ikast   Ebeltoft
Hee   Silkeborg   Århus
Ringkøbing Videbæk   147m   Marselisborg Slot
Ringkøbing Skjern Brande Skanderborg Forhistorisk
Fjord   Tarm   Odder Museum Moesgård
Tipperne   Give   Hov Nordby
Naturreservat Grindsted Legoland Jelling Horsens Sælvig Samsø
Varde   Billund Vejle Juelsminde Tranebjerg
Marbæk   Rands Ford Vejle Fjord Endelave Kalundborg
Esbjerg   Vejen Fredericia
Nordby Bramming Kolding Middelfart Sjælland
Fanø Fanø   Geografisk   Sjælland
Sønderho Ribe Gram Have Fyn Odense
Bugt Mandø   Haderslev Arø Assens Nyborg
Rømø   Vojens
Toftlund   Fåborg
Bredebro Løgumkloster Aabenraa Svendborg
Møgeltønder Draved Als Langeland
Tønder   Skov Tinglev
Sønderborg
Padborg   Ærø   Lolland

D

A strategically placed stork's nest

JUTLAND (JYLLAND)

This aptly named peninsula is about 250 miles (400km) from north to south and boasts an amazing variety of terrain on a miniature scale. The south is marshy grazing land, and dotted with pretty towns whose history is closely linked to that of Schleswig–Holstein in Germany. Many market towns maintain their strong cattle-raising tradition and still hold cattle fairs and tilting tournaments.

Mid-Jutland's landscape includes lakes and moors inland, and on the coast, wide beaches of white sand and lagoons. Off the tapering northern tip of Denmark (the Skaw) is the unusual spectacle of two seas colliding. Here the wind has created sand dunes and beaches along the coast. In this ancient part of Europe, human influence on the landscape dates back to the Stone Age, and Viking graves, Bronze Age burial mounds and re-created homesteads may be seen. Three of Denmark's largest towns are on Jutland, but their total population is still less than half a million people.

WHAT TO SEE

◆◆◆
BILLUND

Billund is a small village dominated by the airport, **Legoland** (see page 51) and the **Museumscenter Billund**, both within walking distance of the airport. The latter is a huge white building housing a trio of transport collections:

The **Danmarks Flyvemuseum** (Aviation Museum) covers 80 years of aviation and includes Ellehammer's aeromachine (1906) and information on the development of aircraft engines, space research and meteorology.

The **Danmarks Bilmuseum** (Car Museum) exhibits over 70 gleaming cars and a good collection of motor cycles. Denmark's own car pioneer, Jørgen Skafte Rasmussen, who founded DKW, has a special stand.

The **Falck Museet**, named after its founder, shows past and present rescue equipment used by the fire and ambulance services. Frogmen and firemen give demonstrations.

◆◆
CLAUSHOLM

Clausholm Slot (Clausholm Castle) is a five-winged baroque mansion built at the beginning of the 18th century for the Lord Chancellor, Count Conrad Reventlow. His daughter Anna Sophie eloped with Frederik IV and became Queen; after his death in 1730 she lived at Clausholm with her court.

The richly furnished rooms have elaborate stucco ceilings and decorated panels. In the chapel is Denmark's oldest organ. The extensive grounds include a number of fountains. The castle lies southeast of Randers.

◆◆
EBELTOFT
The name means 'apple orchard' and apple trees still flourish in this charming seaside market town, one of the most attractive in Denmark. Long, cobbled streets parallel to the shore are lined with timber-framed houses, many over 200 years old. Several are now shops, and while the pottery, patchwork and picture shops fit easily into this rural setting, those selling videos, sportswear and milkshakes seem incongruous.

Sightseeing
Ebeltoft has a long history and claims its 16th-century **Det gamle Rådhus** (old town hall) holds the smallest museum in the world. In summer two uniformed nightwatchmen, with spiked mace and lantern, sing old songs on the town hall steps. The church dates from the 13th century and has many ancient frescoes. **Den gamle Farvergård** (the old dyeworks), with shop and dyehouse, has also been converted into a museum. In contrast, the **Glasmuseum** (Glass Museum), in the former Custom House, shows modern pieces made by over 400 international glass-makers, and demonstrations are given in summer.

On the coast are three harbours – for fishing, for yachts and for other trade – and also a ferry service to Zealand (1 hour 40 minutes to Sjællands Odde). The major coastal attraction is the *Jylland*, the world's largest wooden sail-carrying warship, launched in 1860 and now restored.

The sea-based **Windmill Park** is unusual: the windmills generate enough energy to supply about 600 houses and attract many visitors.

The beaches in **Ebeltoft Bay** are safe, sandy and clean and the area is suitable for windsurfing and fishing.

A fleet of fishing boats moored at Esbjerg port

Accommodation

Several hotels have apartments or bungalows, in which you must stay for at least a week. Such is the central **Hotel Vigen** (tel: 86 34 48 00). The larger and dearer **Hvide Hus** (tel: 86 34 14 66) and **Ebeltoft Strand** (tel: 86 34 33 00) both overlook the sea. All have indoor pools. Near the Windmill Park is **Ebeltoft Maritime Ferieby Øer** (tel: 86 34 00 00), a holiday village of 300 bungalows. Among the facilities are a sports hall, swimming pool, marina, shops and restaurants.

Restaurants

Two restaurants in the main street specialise in Danish food: **Ane Kirstine** and **Mellem Jyder**, in a half-timbered building with a garden.

ESBJERG

The ice-free port of Esbjerg is the largest and most modern fishing port in Scandinavia. Britons coming to Denmark with their cars land at Esbjerg, and although there may be a strong whiff near the fish factory if the wind blows onshore, it's worth spending at least half a day here to see the Fishery Museum and the shops. Esbjerg was built around the turn of the century in the so-called 'American' period, designed on a grid pattern with a motley collection of towers and spires. A special ticket gives you museum entry, a motorboat tour of the harbours and includes a visit to the restored **Vandtårn** (Water Tower), which offers fine views.

Sightseeing

A visit to the **Fiskeri-og Søfartsmuseum** (Fisheries and Maritime Museum), 2 miles (3km) north of Esbjerg is fascinating. Split into four parts, the **Fishery Exhibition** shows old fishing equipment and boats, rescued and carefully restored. Some unusual aspects of fishing are described, such as old eel-trade routes and the demise of the sailing cutter. In the **Maritime Open-Air Exhibition**, set on sand dunes, are fishing boats, wrecks, fishermen's huts, a life-boat station and harbour. Playful seals inhabit the large **Sealarium**, while 50 species of Danish fish and shellfish live in the **Saltvandsakvariet** (Salt Water Aquarium).

The **Esbjerg Museum/ Vestjylllands Ravmuseum** (West Jutland Amber Museum) is two museums in one. The first displays Viking finds, but chiefly focuses on local history from 1890–1940, with realistic streets and buildings, and the other traces the story of amber which is found all along this part of the coast.

The **Esbjerg Kunstmuseum** (Art Museum) is devoted to Danish artists and sculptors from 1920. At Fanø ferry harbour, visit the old lightship *Horns Rev*.

Accommodation

The centrally located **Britannia** (tel: 75 13 01 11) is modern and reasonably priced. The **Hermitage Hotel West** (tel: 75 13 55 00), on American motel lines, is set in a deer park 2 miles (3km) from the centre. A cheaper hotel in town is the **Park Hotel** (tel: 75 12 08 68).

Restaurants

Good-value food is available at
Restaurant Bourgogne on
Skolegade and **Restaurant
Kunstpavillonen** (Havnegåde
20), in the Art Museum building
(tel: 75 12 64 95). **Sand's
Restaurant** is the oldest in
Esbjerg (Skolegade 60), and
Café Danmark is traditionally
furnished.

Entertainment

Many cafés and restaurants
offer live music – folk, rock or
jazz – and discos stay open late.
Concerts are held in the
modern **Multihuset** and in the
open-air **Byparken** in summer.
English and Irish visitors will
feel at home in the many pubs.

Excursions from Esbjerg

About 7 miles (12km) north of
Esbjerg is the **Marbæk Nature
Reserve**, where marked paths
across sand dunes and woods
lead to Iron Age remains.

FYRKAT

This is the smallest of the Viking
ring forts (see box), thought to
have been built around AD 980
and used for about 20 years.
Made of wood and stacked
turves, the fort had dry moats
on two sides, and four
gateways. The ramparts and
ring fort have been re-created
and the post holes filled in to
outline the former position of
streets and houses.
Inside the circular rampart
were 16 houses, in groups of
four round a courtyard. A
similar three-roomed wooden
Viking longhouse has been built
outside the ramparts, its roof
covered with oak chips. About
50 people would have lived
here, sleeping on low benches
along the walls. There is a
central fireplace and it is
thought that the smoke
dispersed through louvres in
the gables. There is evidence
that the buildings were
destroyed in a fire after the
inhabitants had left. A
storehouse has also been built,
and a new settlement of nine
houses will show the living
conditions of the Viking
peasant.
Outside the fort is a small burial
ground where skeletons of
women and children have been
found, some accompanied by
gifts they were given to take to
the next world. Finds from the
site are on view at the **Hobro
Museum**. 'Viking' activities take
place in summer and a Viking
play is performed.

Viking Forts

It is thought that the Danish king
Harald Bluetooth ordered the
defences at Fyrkat to be built.
The structural accuracy of this
site – 394 feet (exactly 120m) in
diameter, and equal spacing
between the houses – shows a
high level of technical skills.
The Vikings' four Danish
strongholds, at Trelleborg,
Aggersborg, Nonnebakken and
Fyrkat were all military centres,
and were probably bases for
westward expeditions.
At Fyrkat, few weapons have
been found, but spindles and
warps, goldsmiths' melting pots
and items of jewellery indicate
that the Vikings also led a
peaceful domestic existence.

Replica Viking longhouse at Fyrkat

◆◆
GAMMEL ESTRUP
Jyllands Herregårdsmuseum
(Jutland Manor House Museum)
and **Dansk Landbrugsmuseum**
(Danish Agricultural Museum)
are two good reasons for
visiting this attractive house in
rural Djursland. Gammel Estrup
is near the village of Auning, on
the road between Grenå and
Randers.

The manor house itself is a fine,
moated, Renaissance castle and
the earliest part was built
towards the end of the 15th
century. It was inhabited by two
noble families, once political
advisors to the Danish royal
family. Their descendants
founded the museum, which
contains their heirlooms and
family portraits.

Its rooms are elegant, with
painted ceilings, French and
English furniture and porcelain.
A 17th-century turret wall has
been plastered in a style to
imitate drapery.

The Agricultural Museum is in a
separate building in the

grounds. It was founded over a
century ago and houses a
collection of over 25,000
agricultural implements. A
permanent exhibition of farm
interiors illustrates two
centuries of Danish country life.
In summer children can try out
for themselves old farming
methods such as threshing with
a flail or grinding corn, and the
local Guild of Blacksmiths gives
demonstrations. There are
pleasant gardens and a café.
Energetic visitors can hire a
canoe from Sjellebro by
contacting the tourist office at
Auning (tel: 86 48 34 44).

◆
HERNING
This modern town is the centre
of the Danish textile industry
and hosts international trade
fairs at its exhibition complex. It
also has some good museums
and outstanding art collections
and is also popular with anglers
for its sea trout.

Sightseeing

The **Herning Museum** (Museumsgade 28) holds the main collection of finds from Central Jutland. Also included are paintings of the Jutland landscape and an unusual collection of Danish country scenes (Jens Nielsen's farm) of the 1920s which are set in small boxes, producing a type of three-dimensional diorama. Outside are typical Jutland buildings. Next door is the **Danmarks Fotomuseum** (Photographic Museum), which shows the development of techniques during the last century. The huge panoramic photo of Copenhagen should not be missed. The museum holds exhibitions of work by both Danish and foreign photographers.

Two modern art collections lie one mile (2km) east of the town. **Carl-Henning Pedersen and Else Alfelt's Museum** feature over 4,000 works of art by this couple, and 100 yards (90m) of outside walls are covered with brightly coloured ceramic slabs. Close by is the **Herning Kunstmuseum** (Art Museum) and a sculpture park with works dating from the 1950s, by international and Danish artists. Beyond are **De Geometriske Haver** (the Geometrical Gardens).

The town's oldest building, the imposing manor house of **Herningsholm** (1579), is now a museum of the Jutland-born poet Steen Steensen Blicher (1782–1848). The painted ceilings and murals bring to life the poet's manuscripts and memorabilia.

KOLDING

In 1268 **Koldinghus Castle** was built on a rocky bluff by the Danish King Erik V as a fortress against the Duchy of Schleswig. Later monarchs added towers and chapels and rebuilt the fortress as a castle. After a chequered history of fire, military occupation and abandonment, the castle was rebuilt in 1890. Today **Museet på Koldinghus** is a lakeside museum, the oldest part dating from the 15th century.

A visit to this red-brick castle provides good exercise, for access from one wing to another is often only possible by descending to the courtyard and climbing up again. The museum is crammed with Gothic and Romanesque church sculpture, heavy oak furniture, relics from the Schleswig Wars, Chinese porcelain, European pictures and interiors dating from the 16th century onwards.

In the impressive Ruin Hall, original brick pillars are protected under a light roof, this is supported by new wooden pillars and linked to a high-tech gallery to re-create the original dimensions. A colony of Pipistrelle bats lives in the church.

Other sights in Kolding include the old timbered pharmacy, the **Borchs Gård** and the later neo-Romanesque town hall. The **Kunstmuseet Trapholt**, in a park overlooking the fjord, is a modern art museum, displaying Expressionist art and the best of Danish design in furniture, china and textiles.

This windmill at Skagen is thatched

500 BC, discovered in a nearby peatbog during the last century. A half-timbered merchant's house now accomodates the Tourist Office with **Den Smidste Gård** above. This museum traces the town's 800-year history with unusual finds, from the contents of Viking tombs to domestic utensils buried during the Swedish Wars. The **Vejle Museum** displays local archaeological finds, and next door is the **Vejle Kunstmuseum** (Art Museum), with one of Denmark's best collections of modern graphics, paintings and sculpture.

Accommodation

The large **Munkebjerg Hotel** (tel: 75 72 35 00), 4 miles (6km) outside the town, is expensive, with sizeable grounds and a casino. In town is the reasonably priced family **Park Hotel** (tel: 75 82 24 66). The **Dan Inn Hotel** (tel: 75 88 17 77), west of Vejle, has a garden.

Restaurants

In Torvenhallerne, the indoor market hall, are several eating places. Or, try Baghushet or Bone's in Daemingen.

Excursions from Vejle

On the southern side of the fjord, there are sandy beaches at Andkær Vig bay and around Hvidbjerg/Mørkholt with its extensive dunes.

Jelling is well worth seeing, and has some amazing monuments marking important events in Danish history. Two large mounds in the village centre are thought to be the burial places of the Viking King Gorm and his Queen, Thyra, who died around AD 935. Outside the whitewashed church are two rune stones erected as monuments to them. The **Great Rune Stone**, erected by their son, Harald Bluetooth, has been called Denmark's baptismal certificate as its inscriptions recall Denmark's unification, its adoption of Christianity and the conquest of Norway. The church, on the site of a much larger wooden one built by Harald, contains old frescoes, a chambered tomb and various ornaments thought to have belonged to King Gorm. Legend has it that Harald reburied his pagan father in the church after his (Harald's) conversion to Christianity. **Randbøl Hede** moor is another pretty place to visit. History buffs should see **Ravning Bridge** (1,000 years old), the **Egtved Girl's Grave** (her body is in the National Museum) and the **Old Military Road**. This is the old medieval military and trade route (*Hærvejen*) which ran between Jutland and Schleswig Holstein in Germany.

VIBORG

Viborg can trace its history back to the eighth century when pagans worshiped here; later the advent of Christianity brought a cathedral (AD 1130) and a bishop's see, and Danish kings were crowned here up until 1655.

The town sits astride two lakes and its location in the centre of Jutland made it an important trading centre. Much of the original architecture was destroyed in two great fires, in 1567 and 1726. Today it is a market town, with a small historic centre and some fine old houses, especially along Skt Mogensgade.

Sightseeing

Viborg is dominated by its twin towered **cathedral**, but only the crypt survives from the original building. The rest was rebuilt during the last century in Romanesque style. The most striking interior features are richly-coloured murals of biblical scenes, by Joakim Skovgaard, who also painted the ceilings. A quiet public

garden outside the west door, the **Latinerhaven** (Latin Garden), once belonged to the Latin master at the cathedral school. In the old town hall is the **Skovgaard Museum** exhibiting a variety of craftwork – silver, furniture, bookbinding, paintings – by three generations of the Skovgaard family and their friends. Joakim's sketchbooks with preliminary drawings for the cathedral are included. The **Stiftsmuseum** (District Museum) in Hjultorvet portrays the town's history in thematic displays of workshops.

Accommodation and Restaurants

The **Golf Hotel Viborg** (tel: 86 61 02 22) is a long, low building in a beautiful lakeside setting. Just 5 miles (8km) southeast is **Rindsholm Kro** (tel: 86 63 90 44), a small comfortable inn with a garden. It is renowned for its good food.

Two good restaurants are in Skt Mathias Gade: **Latinerly** (at 78) with basement café and **Messing Jens** (at 48).

Excursions from Viborg

West of Viborg are two fascinating limestone mines (*kalkgruber*). The **Mønsted mines** were worked for 1,000 years and are the largest in Denmark, with 25 miles (40km) of galleries, up to 65 feet (20m) high, which now provide a cool home for thousands of bats. The mines are also used for limestone and bat museums, cheese storage (about 200 tons of it!) and the occasional classical concert. **Daugbjerg** is older, smaller and darker.

◆
AALBORG (ÅLBORG)

This modern, vibrant city is the
fourth largest in Denmark and
lies on the southern bank of the
Limfjord. Its wealth is now
based on the manufacture of
cement and aquavit, no longer
on herring and tobacco.
Aalborg can trace its history
back to the Vikings, and in 1992
celebrated 1,300 years since
they first settled near by. Much
of the town has been rebuilt
since the war, but although tall
glass and concrete structures
now dwarf the clusters of older
buildings, there are still some
attractive areas with fine 17th-
century and half-timbered
houses, some relocated from
other streets (the junction at
Nørregade and Fjordgade is a
particularly good example).

Aa-h!

In the Danish alphabet, aa is
replaced by å. However, the
town of Aalborg prefers to keep
this spelling. In an alphabetical
listing of towns, you will still find
it at the end, after Z, along with
all the Ås.

Sightseeing

The **Jens Bangs Stenhus**, at
Østerå-Gade 9, is an ornate five-
storey brick house with unusual
curved gables, built in 1624 by
a local merchant, Jens Bang. It is
claimed to be Scandinavia's
largest private house from the
Renaissance, and stands close
to the baroque Rådhus (Town
Hall), built around 1760. The
gargoyles are said to represent
councillors of Bang's day who
would not elect him. Today the

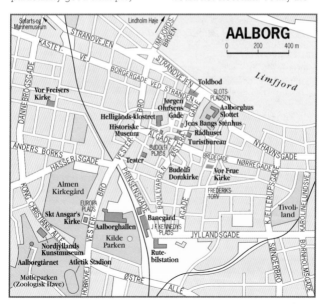

Gargoyle at the Jens Bangs Stenhus

building is a pharmacy (as it has been for 300 years), and the vaulted cellar is a popular wine bar.

Vestiges of earlier occupation can be seen in the **Aalborg Historiske Museum** (Historical Museum), which displays many items dating from the Stone Age and fine examples of glass from later periods. One of its treasures is the 1602 Aalborg Room which was removed from a merchant's home and reconstructed here. It is panelled in richly carved oak with a frieze of biblical quotations and has a coffered ceiling.

The **Budolfi Domkirke** (St Botolph's Cathedral) is a whitewashed brick edifice in Gothic style, built around 1400, with a later baroque spire. It has a carved pulpit, large altarpiece and some early frescoes.

The **Helligåndsklostret** (the Monastery of the Holy Ghost) is a red-brick, step-gabled building almost the same age as Budolfi. A former nunnery and monastery, it was dedicated to the care of the ill and elderly, work which continues today. It is Denmark's

oldest social institution (1431) and visitors can go on conducted tours to see the monks' refectory and the frescoes on the chapel ceiling. The **Aalborghus Slot** is a white, step-gabled building near the harbour. Built in the 16th century as a fortress by King Christian III, it never served this purpose but instead became the residence of the king's representative. Now visitors can tour the dungeons, casemates and ramparts.

The **Aalborg Søfartsog Marinemuseum** (Aalborg Maritime Museum) is situated near the west end of the harbour. Displays inside and out give visitors a picture of sailors' lives in the early days of seafaring. You can go inside Denmark's last submarine, *Springeren* and torpedo boat *Søbjørnen*. Part of the museum is devoted to the town's shipbuilding industry.

The **Nordjyllands Kunstmuseum** (North Jutland Museum of Modern and Contemporary Art) is in an outstanding modern structure (designed by Finnish architects Elissa and Alvar Aalto, with Danish architect Jean-Jaques Baruël), built 1968–72 and set in a large woodland area. The museum has a permanent collection of Danish and foreign art dating from the end of the last century, and a children's museum. The sculpture park is dominated by the glass pyramid *Dream Palace* by Bjørn Nørgaard, and an amphitheatre where music and variety shows are staged.

Close by is the **Aalborgtårnet** (Aalborg Tower), 344 feet (105m) above sea level, which gives a fine view of the town and the fjord (there is a lift). Other attractions are: the **Zoo** in Mølleparkens – one of the biggest in northern Europe where animals are free to roam; **Vandland**, a large indoor tropical water park, and **Tivoliland**, a huge amusement park with a Chinatown and over 80 attractions.

Transport

City sightseeing tours (with English commentary) lasting over two hours start from Adelgade on summer weekdays at 11.00hrs.

Accommodation

For a central hotel try the new **Chagall** (tel: 98 12 69 33), or the **Slotshotellet** near the waterfront (tel: 98 10 14 00). In a parkland setting is the recently renovated **Hotel Hvide Hus** (tel: 98 13 84 00), with a 15th-floor restaurant. The **Park Hotel** (tel: 98 12 31 33) near the station is cheaper.

Restaurants

There are over 300 restaurants in Aalborg which is often dubbed 'Little Paris of the North'. Jomfru Ane Gade is a pretty and popular pedestrian-only street, with Denmark's longest continuous stretch of pubs and restaurants. **Restaurant Dufy** at 6–8 is situated in an old house. At 21 is **Restaurant Faklen** which serves international food to a high standard. For fish, try the more expensive **Penny Lane Fish Restaurant**, at Sankelmarksgade 9.

Entertainment

Aalborg is second only to Copenhagen for its nightlife. Many restaurants and pubs, particularly around Jomfru Ane Gade, offer jazz, rock and folk music, as well as dancing and billiards. For highbrow entertainment, the modern **Aalborghallen** (Congress and Cultural Centre) hosts visiting performers of the arts and orchestras from abroad. Aalborg Symphony Orchestra has its own auditorium here and there are exhibition halls and conference facilities.

Excursions from Aalborg

Lindholm Høje, north of Limfjord at Nørresundby is the largest Viking burial site in Scandinavia totalling 150 ship-shaped stones, interspersed with about 700 graves and smaller stones from later Iron Age settlers. Cremated bodies were interred with burial objects, and the better are now on show in the museum, which also has tableaux depicting how the tribes lived as traders and explorers.

♦♦♦
ÅRHUS ✓

Århus, on Jutland's east coast, is Denmark's second largest city, well situated for visitors who want to savour both coast and countryside. The city is fortunate in having several swathes of greenery around it. Culture thrives here with a dozen museums, several small theatres and an exciting modern concert hall.

A tenth of the town's quarter of a million population are students, who help to create the liveliest music scene in Denmark. An international jazz festival is held each July, and an arts festival in September. Århus's valley situation and proximity to the sea encouraged the Vikings to settle here a thousand years ago. As a trading centre the town flourished, but in the Middle Ages the population fell

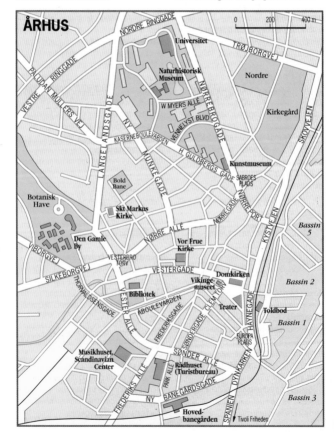

dramatically as a result of wars and the Black Death. Århus is once again a prosperous city, with some well-designed modern buildings and a cluster of old ones found around the cathedral, which has now become a popular café area.

Sightseeing

The **Domkirken** (St Clemen's cathedral) is Denmark's longest church. A Romanesque basilica was built in 1200, but was destroyed by fire and rebuilt in Gothic style in the late 15th century. Note the vault by the pre-Reformation Lübeck master craftsman Bernt Notke, and the modern, painted glass window by the Norwegian Emmanuel Vigeland.

Viking remains found near the cathedral show that this part of the city has always been the centre of the Århus community. The old walls which surrounded the Viking town, a typical dwelling and some tools can all be seen at the site of the excavation, in the basement of Unibank, at Clemens Torv, now the **Vikingemuseet** (Viking Museum).

Northwest of the cathedral, along Vestergåde, stands the Gothic 13th-century **Vor Frue Kirke** (Church of Our Lady), within which are ruins of an earlier stone crypt church (AD 1060). The main church has frescoes and a fine altarpiece by Claus Berg (1520). The Gothic cloister leads to the former chapter house, now an old people's home; its walls are covered with well-preserved medieval secular paintings. Before you leave the centre,

two modern buildings deserve more than a just a passing glance:

The **Århus Rådhus** (City Hall) is a marble-clad structure, with an unusual tower designed by Arne Jacobsen and Erik Møller and built in 1941. Guided tours of the council chamber and civic hall show murals from the days of Nazi occupation, painted by Albert Naur, who managed to include some secret symbols. There is a wonderful view of the city and the bay from the 197-foot (60m) bell tower.

The **Musikhuset** (Concert Hall) was built in 1982 and is the home of the Jutland Opera and Århus Symphony Orchestra. It is a tall glass structure, supported inside by slender white pillars, with palm trees to relieve the yellow brickwork. There are free foyer concerts and art exhibitions.

On the west of Århus is **Den Gamle By** (the Old Town), an open-air museum set in a park. Over 70 houses and workshops, mostly half-timbered, the oldest of which is 500 years old, have been dismantled all over Denmark and rebuilt here to recreate urban life as it used to be, complete with cobbled streets. An authentic atmosphere is created by the opening of the old-fashioned bakers' and grocers' shops. This museum can attract large crowds at the height of summer.

A large part of the park is occupied by the colourful **Botanisk Have** (Botanical Gardens), with its glasshouses and tropical plants.

A large green area north of Århus is occupied by the University and several museums. The **Århus Kunstmuseum** (Art Museum) in Vennelyst Park, displays Danish paintings and sculpture from 1750 and holds regular exhibitions of modern art. The **Steno Museum** (Danish Museum of the History of Science) is a hands-on museum which includes a planetarium and a herb garden. The vast **Naturhistorisk Museum** (Natural History Museum) has a display of stuffed animals and birds in their natural habitats and shows the evolution of, and influences on, Denmark's landscape.

Transport

You can take guided bus tours of Århus and the surrounding countryside: ask at the Tourist Office. With a 24-hour **Tourist Ticket**, you get unlimited travel on town buses and three tours of Århus, while a two- or seven-day **Århus Pas** also includes free entry to most museums. Tickets are sold at hotels, campsites, news stands and the Tourist Office. If you want to travel like a Dane, buy a multi-ride ticket which gives you 11 bus rides on one ticket: remember to punch it each time you get on a bus.

Accommodation

There is a good selection of hotels, both in and out of town. Central and inexpensive is the friendly **Hotel Ritz**, near the railway station (tel: 86 13 44 44); much more expensive is the 150-year-old **Royal** (tel: 86 12 00 11), a classical building which has been luxuriously renovated and now operates the casino. The cheapest hotels in town are **Eriksens** (tel: 86 13 62 96) by the station, and the **Hotel Windsor** (tel: 86 12 23 00). The **Hotel La Tour** (tel: 86 16 78 88) to the north is ideal for families, with comfortable rooms. For a stay on the coast the modern **Hotel Marselis** (tel: 86 14 44 11) on Strandvejen overlooks the sea and benefits from its own swimming pool.

Restaurants

With over 200 places serving food, the choice is wide. **Teater Bodega** (Skolegade 7), with playbills and photos on the walls, is comfortable and serves reliably good food. The unpretentious **Rådhus Kafeen** is good value for such a central location. The **Guldhornet** (near the station at Banegårdspladsen 1) has a good atmosphere and quick service. You can eat outside in the courtyard at **Jacob's Bar BQ** (Vestergade 3). Fish lovers, on the other hand, should head for the **Marselisborg Yacht Harbour** south of Århus and try the **Seafood Restaurant** (tel: 86 18 56 55).

Entertainment

Concerts, operas, plays (in Danish) and ballet alternate in the **Concert Hall**'s two auditoria. The season at the **Århus Theatre** runs from September to June, and there are other small theatres. There are four cinemas with 17

Fine historic buildings are gathered together at Århus Old Town

screens between them. The monthly publication *What's on in Århus*, available from the tourist office, lists events. There are about a dozen venues for rock and jazz: for rock, try **Vestergade 58** and **Musikcafeen** (Mejlgade 53). Jazz is played nightly at **Glazzhuset** (Åboulevarden 35). Several cafés around the cathedral have live music too, with bands or piano bars, while discos and nightclubs are proliferating fast – try **Blitz**, on Klostergade for the over-20s and **Edison Nightclub** (Frederiksgade 76) for the over-23s. **Palmehaven** (Østergade 12) if you are older.

Excursions from Århus

The **Grauballe Man** is Århus' oldest and best-preserved inhabitant, whose Iron Age body, dating from 300 BC was found in a peat bog. His small-featured face is fringed with gingery hair. The body lies in the small **Forhistorisk Museum Moesgård** (Moesgård Prehistoric Museum), about 5 miles (8km) south of the city. Other exhibits include some rune stones. Outside is a trail leading to the sea, passing reconstructed prehistoric dwellings and burial mounds. The large, wooded area south of Århus is **Marselisborg**, the city's playground. The amusement park **Tivoli Friheden** is situated amid flowers and parkland, and live performances take place on the open-air stage. **Marselisborg**

Skov (woods) and **Dyrehaven** (deer park) are crossed with pleasant paths to walk. **Marselisborg Slot** (Marselisborg Castle), the royal family's summer home, is near by. Changing of the guard takes place at noon when the family is in residence; the gardens are open when the family is not there. The **Mindeparken** (War Memorial Park) commemorates South Jutland's losses in World War I. There are good Blue Flag beaches at **Moesgård** and **Ballehage** (near Marselisborg Skov). North of town, you can bathe at **Bellevue** and **den Permanente** beaches. **Kattegatcentret**, near Grenå (40 miles/64km northeast) has sea creatures in glass tanks.

JUTLAND'S ISLANDS

WHAT TO SEE

◆
ANHOLT
This tiny island of 22 square miles (57sq km) lies in the middle of the Kattegat between Denmark and Sweden, and the ferry trip from Grenå takes nearly three hours.
Once occupied by the British Navy during the Napoleonic Wars, today Anholt has around 150 inhabitants.
No cars are permitted and *ørkenen* (drifting sands) are the main feature visible from the low hills at Nordbjerg. Just north of here is a sanctuary for wading birds. The beaches are good and bikes can be hired. For accommmodation, there is one campsite at **Nordstrandvej** (tel: 86 31 91 00).

◆
FANØ
A mere 20-minute ferry ride from Esbjerg, Fanø is 11 miles (18km) long, and the sandy beaches of its west coast tend to draw large crowds. The inhabitants bought the island from King Christian VI when he auctioned it in 1741, and with it came the right to build sailing boats. Some of central Fanø is wooded, and much is covered with holiday homes and campsites.

Sightseeing
In **Nordby**, the **Fanø Skibsfart-og Dragtsamling** (Maritime and Costume Collection) displays model ships and local dress, and at the **Fanø Museum** are artefacts depicting the

islanders' lifestyle over the past 300 years. Model ships are suspended from the ceiling of the 18th-century church. The prettiest village is **Sønderho**, with its windmill, old thatched houses and narrow streets.

Accommodation and Restaurants
There are eight campsites and two holiday centres on Fanø. **Sønderho Kro** (tel: 75 16 40 09) is full of character and serves good food.
Fanø Krogård at Nordby is a cosy 17th-century inn (tel: 75 16 20 52) serving good meals, and you can also eat at **Kellers Hotel** by the sea.
In Sønderho, **Kromanns Fiskerestaurant** (tel: 75 16 44 45) specialises in fish dishes, and at Nordby, **Restaurant Fanø Krogård** is a cosy 17th-century inn (tel: 75 16 20 52).

◆◆
LÆSØ
An hour-and-a-half ferry trip from Frederikshavn on Jutland brings you to Læsø, 44 square miles (114sq km), exactly the same size as Samsø, but with half its population – some 2,550. The ferry lands at Vesterø Havn, where it is met by a bus which takes you 5 miles (8km) to Byrum, the chief town.
The island is ideal for nature-lovers: three quarters of it is wild, with woods, moorland and sand dunes. Wild flowers are abundant and include orchids. In the south are salt marshes, and wading birds live in a group of islets off that coast. Daily visits can be made here by tractor-bus which starts from

Byrum. The Knotten peninsula in the northeast is also a bird sanctuary. The best sandy beaches are on the long north coast and many have been awarded Blue Flags.

Sightseeing

Læsø's most unusual feature without doubt is the seaweed-thatched roofs on many farmhouses in the chief town of **Byrum**. Even the half-timbered **Museumsgården** (local museum), nearly 400 years old, has a seaweed thatch. The tower by the Romanesque church has a view over the whole island. The **Fiskeri-og Søfartsmuseet** (Fishing and Maritime Museum) at Vesterø Havn displays seafaring items and describes the lifestyle of early islanders.

Accommodation

Among the better hotels to aim for are **Lærkely** (tel: 98 49 83 44) located in Byrum and

Safe harbour for yachts on Samsø

Havnebakken (tel: 98 49 90 09) found in Vesterø Havn.

SAMSØ

Situated in the Kattegat, halfway between Jutland, Zealand and Funen, Samsø is a delightfully rural, bottle-shaped island, particularly rich in birdlife. White churches and small villages with thatched cottages are scattered over the island. The inland scenery ranges from moors to forest, while the coast offers cliffs and sandy beaches. There is much rich farmland which is intensively cultivated. The potatoes are reputed to be the best in Denmark and, in late summer, the trusting residents put trays of local produce outside their houses for sale. Samsø is a popular holiday resort and many homes are rented out for the summer, including the thatched ones. The island is easily accessible from Hov on Jutland to Sælvig (1 hour 20 minutes on the ferry) or

from Kalundborg on Zealand to Kolby Kås (2 hours). You can hire a bicycle at Sælvig and at Kolby Kås to explore the island, or you can catch the bus, which meets the ferry and stops at many different places.

Sightseeing

The chief town is **Tranebjerg**, with little of note except a 14th-century church, and a large defence tower with holes from which tar and hot water were poured on invaders in the Middle Ages. The **museum** illustrates life on the island down the ages.

Nordby is a captivating village where the half-timbered cottages, stand higgledy-piggledy. The church is half a mile (1km) away – the villages it served are long since abandoned – so Nordby has a separate bell tower. Tracks lead to the beach, or you can go further north to **Nordby Bakker**, a nature reserve, with marked walks. **Ballebjerg** is the highest point on Samsø, with good views from its lookout tower. **Besser Rev**, on the east, is a reef encircling the lagoon of Stavns Fjord, now a bird reserve. Other sights include a restored post mill at Brundby, and the 15th-century church at Onsbjerg with a gold crucifix dating from around 1200.

Accommodation and Restaurants

Flinchs Hotel at Tranebjerg (tel: 86 59 17 22) has been tastefully renovated and serves good food. **Nordby Kro**, in Nordby (tel: 86 59 60 86), is a cottage-style building with a restaurant.

BORNHOLM

Bornholm has belonged to Denmark since 1658, when much of southern Sweden was under Danish rule. The island lies 95 miles (153km) southeast of Copenhagen – a seven-hour ferry trip to Rønne, the main town. Bornholm is rhomboid in shape and larger than many other islands, but still only 25 miles (40km) between its most distant corners. It consists of granite which gives rise to rugged coastal cliffs; the **Heligsdomsklipperne** is the most spectacular formation northwest of Gudhjem. The mild climate produces unusual fauna and flora, and the island is a stopover for migrating birds. Bornholm has sandy beaches, villages with half-timbered houses and several fortified churches. Prehistoric remains include burial mounds, passage graves and rune stones. Potters, glassblowers and artists have been drawn to Bornholm by its beauty; their creations are sold in many galleries and workshops. Golf and cycling are popular here.

WHAT TO SEE

Rønne, the main town, is full of tiny dark red or ochre-coloured half-timbered houses lining

Fish Trade
Bornholm has always been an important trading centre and today's islanders earn their living from fishing and fish processing – the **Bornholmer**, a smoked herring, is highly recommended.

A typical round church on Bornholm

narrow cobbled streets round the lively harbour. The **Bornholm Museum** displays a collection of local prehistoric and geological finds, as well as an old grocer's shop, toys, costumes, clocks and ceramics. The **Art Museum** in the same building has paintings from c.1800. **Erichsens Gård** is an early 19th-century furnished merchant's house with garden. The smallest of the island's four round churches is at **Nylars**, with frescoes round the top of the central pillar and a rune stone in the porch. **Hasle**, site of the annual herring festival, is another quaint village, with a **Smokehouse Museum**. The 13th-century **Hammershus Castle**, once Scandinavia's largest fortress, is now an impressive, overgrown red-brick ruin of towers and turrets. Beyond is the huge **Hammeren boulder**. **Sandvig** and **Allinge** are two medieval fishing villages with narrow, twisting streets and busy harbours. Sandvig also has a wide, sandy beach. At **Madsebakke** is a group of old rock carvings.

The road descends steeply to **Gudhjem** (ferries go from here to the island of **Christiansø**, a former naval base) which still has some smokehouses. Just beyond, at Melsted, is **Melstedgård**, where 18th- and 19th-century half-timbered farm buildings together form a living agricultural museum, featuring demonstrations of traditional farming methods. At **Østerlars** is the largest of the round churches, at Nylars, the best preserved and at Ols, the tallest.

Svaneke is a prosperous market town with an attractive harbour. At **Dueodde** is the island's best and largest beach, part of a large dune area backed by pinewoods. The sand is so fine it is used in egg-timers; once it was sold as 'writers' sand', to dry ink. There are numerous campsites and holiday homes here. Inland at **Åkirkeby**, the island's oldest market town, is a 12th-century stone church with impressive Romanesque carving on the sandstone font.

Accommodation

The **Hotel Griffen** in Rønne (tel: 56 95 51 11) is comfortable and central. At Svaneke, try the small **Pension Solgården** (tel: 56 49 64 37) with harbour view and garden. In Dueodde, **Hotel Bornholm** (tel: 56 48 83 83) has its own pools. Accommodation is also available in private houses, but you may have to stay for a minimum time, usually three days.

ZEALAND (SJÆLLAND)

This is Denmark's biggest and most densely populated island where much of Danish industry is situated. North Zealand has some spectacular castles which are easy to visit from Copenhagen. The coast is sandy, but public beaches near the capital tend to get crowded. The southern part of Zealand is more rural and includes some historic towns.

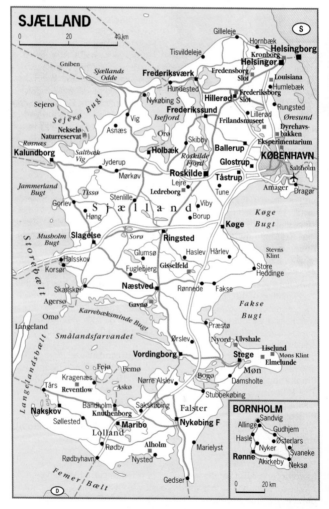

WHAT TO SEE

◆◆◆
FREDERIKSBORG SLOT ✓
(FREDERIKSBORG CASTLE)

At **Hillerød**, is a fairy-tale castle built (1602–20) on three islands by Christian IV, with an excess of spires, gables and copper-green roofs. He demolished the previous castle on the site, which had been built in 1560 by his father, Frederik II as a hunting base. A large part of Christian's castle was burnt down during the last century and the present castle is a faithful reconstruction of his original masterpiece.

In 1878 it became home to **Det Nationalhistoriske Museum** (the National Historical Museum), covering 500 years of Danish history.

The castle's years of glory were between 1671 and 1840, when it was the home of all Danish monarchs, who were crowned in the chapel. Its 60 rooms contain a superb collection of paintings, furniture and tapestries by the best European painters and craftspeople of their day. The most magnificent rooms include the huge Riddersalen (Knights' Hall), with a richly decorated vaulted ceiling supported by marble columns, and the splendid Great Hall or Audience Chamber, every inch decorated with gold.

The original chapel wing was designed for royal use, so the most valuable materials were used: the nave vaults are gilded and the king's pew is inlaid with rare woods.

The black marble gallery served as the knights' chapel, and is hung with rows of shields. The ebony ceiling in the royal oratories is decorated with ivory rosettes. Even the smaller rooms are richly and tastefully decorated and filled with antiques.

The lovely gardens which surround the castle and the lake are also well worth seeing.

The ornate ceiling of the Great Hall is echoed in floor and wall décor

Helsingør is still a major ferry port

◆◆◆
HELSINGØR

Helsingør's early prosperity was based on its position at the neck of the Øresund, which separates Denmark from Sweden. From 1427 until 1857 all of the ships passing through had to pay dues to the ruler of the Sound. Many rich merchants settled here, and the grid-patterned streets lined with charming half-timbered houses still stand.

Sightseeing

Helsingør is Elsinore, home of Shakespeare's Hamlet, who was probably named after the Danish mythological figure, Amleth. **Kronborg Castle**, in a dramatic coastal setting overlooking Øresund, was built on the earlier foundations of a small fortress; it still retains huge bastions and medieval ramparts. Kronborg owes its Dutch Renaissance appearance to King Frederik II who rebuilt it (1574–85); it was again restored in the 1920s. The royal apartments are sparsely

furnished with early, heavy Dutch and Danish pieces, and there is no comfort in the bare floors and stone staircases, but the ceilings are painted and valuable oil paintings and Flemish tapestries cover the walls. The empty, oak-beamed Great Hall is one of the largest in Europe; its walls are hung with scenes of Kronborg by the 17th-century painter Isaac Isaacsz.

The chapel survived a fire in 1629 – its rich carvings and gilded wood contrast with the white vaulted ceiling.

Guided tours of the casemates reveal them to be dark, dank and cobbled. Here sits the statue of **Holger Danske**, Denmark's national hero, a Viking contemporary of the Emperor Charlemagne, said to have fought in the French wars, who, legend has it, will rise again in Denmark's hour of need. At one time the casemates housed a brewery, and the horse and wagon area are still visible.

Even deeper below ground is a former prison, full of bats, and a huge room vast enough to store six weeks' provisions for 1,000 soldiers.

Walk round the bastions before you go – soldiers guard the cannons from their sentry boxes – and remember that this was where the ghost of Hamlet's father trod.

The **Handels-og Søfartsmuseet** (Trade and Maritime Museum) is also at Kronborg (castle ticket admits you). Its large collection on several floors tells the story

of the Danish merchant fleet
and trade with the colonies
from 1400, by showing model
and full-size ships, a stoker's
room and some old navigation
equipment.
In the 15th century three
monasteries were founded at
Helsingør, and the large red-
brick Carmelite building of **Skt
Mariæ**, where the composer
Dietrich Buxtehude was
organist, is said to be the best-
preserved medieval monastery
in northern Europe. The small
Carmelite hospital for seamen
is now the **Helsingør Bymuseum**
(Town Museum), with locally
found items from medieval
times and a unique model of the
town from 1801. **Skt Olai Kirke**
(St Olav's Church), dates from
the same era and features a
magnificent altarpiece.

Accommodation and Restaurants

Hotel Hamlet (with Restaurant
Ophelia!) is comfortable and
near the castle (tel: 49 21 05
91). **Klostercafeen** is good for
lunch, and for dinner **Anno
1880** is a half-timbered house
near Kronborg (tel: 49 21 54
80). There are several eating
places along Stengåde.

Crossing to Sweden
The boat trip to Sweden
(Helsingborg) from Helsingør
takes only 25 minutes (there are
two or three departures every
hour). Don't be surprised to see
lots of Swedes in Helsingør –
they are there to take advantage
of Denmark's cheaper food and
drink, particularly meat, cheese
and alcohol.

Excursions from Helsingør

Completed in 1776,
Fredensborg (Castle of Peace)
is an example of Danish rococo
architecture, built by Frederik
IV to celebrate the end of the
war with Sweden in 1720.
Appropriately, it is in grand
country house style rather than
fortified, and is now used by
the royal family in spring and
autumn. A few rooms are open
to the public in July, but its
extensive park and gardens,
on the edge of Esrum Sø,
Denmark's second biggest
lake, are open all year.
Marienlyst Slot (Castle), stands
north of Helsingør station. First
built as a retreat (*lundehave*)
for Frederik II, it was
redesigned in 1760 for the
widow of Frederik V by the
French architect N H Jardin.
Original Louis XVI interiors with
period furniture fill the top floor,
and there are lovely collections
of paintings and silver. Hamlet's
grave is in the garden.

◆
KALUNDBORG

Kalundborg is better known for
its radio transmitter and its
ferry port to Århus than for its
well-preserved medieval centre
and outstanding 12th-century
church. The **Vor Frue Kirke**
(Church of Our Lady) is shaped
like a Greek cross, with five brick
towers, each topped by a copper
spire. Other medieval buildings
include **Den Gamle Tiendelade**
(the Old Tithe Barn), the Gothic
Borgerhus (Citizen's House) and
some restored small houses.
The **Kalundborg-og Omegns
Museum** (Museum of
Kalundborg and the Environs)

is housed in Lindegaarden, a large, half-timbered building dating from the 16th century, which holds a good collection of local costumes, craftsmen's tools and farmhouse interiors.

Accommodation and Restaurants

Ole Lunds Gård (tel: 53 51 01 65) is central, with a restaurant; near the station is **Restaurant Fjorden** with Café Vigen. **Bromølle Kro** (tel: 53 55 00 90) is an old thatched inn at Jyderup, south of the town.

KØGE

Køge is a charming town with a cobbled market square and many medieval houses and courtyards.

Originally founded in the 13th century as a port, exporting grain to the Baltic towns, Køge prospered in the Middle Ages. But, in the early 17th century fires and the war against Sweden ravaged the town and its population. The old harbour is still used for trade and ship repairs but a new marina has been built 1¼ miles (2km) north.

Sightseeing

The roads leading from the **Torvet** (the market square) are lined with half-timbered houses built after the last fire in 1663; the oldest dated house in Denmark (1527) is at **Kirkestræde 20**.

Skt Nikolai Kirke (St Nicholas Church) with Gothic-style brickwork, has a medieval fresco and many painted epitaphs. From the tower is a view of roofscapes and the bay.

The **Køge Museum**, situated in a range of 17th-century half-timbered buildings round a courtyard, displays locally excavated items such as coins, as well as embroidery and utensils, and two typically furnished living rooms from the 1800s and 1900s.

Accommodation

Hotel Niels Juel (tel: 56 63 18 00) is a new hotel, built in warehouse style, overlooking the harbour, and **Søvilla Kro and Motel** (tel: 53 66 15 14) lies north of the town.

Restaurants

Richters, in Vestergade, (tel: 53 66 29 49) is timber-framed with a courtyard, while modern and airy **Arken** (tel: 53 66 05 05) overlooks the bay.

LOUISIANA MUSEUM

The **Louisiana Museum for Moderne Kunst** (Museum of Modern Art) at Humlebæk is a clever combination of art, sculpture and landscape, based on the collection of art-lover Knud Jensen. The museum is housed in a beautiful hilltop villa and park, with several sculptures some metal, some by Henry Moore, dotted around lawns sloping down to the Øresund. The pictures, dating from the 1950s, are by artists within the CoBrA (see page 57) and Constructivist movements. A new underground Graphic Art wing joins the two existing buildings. American artists, such as Roy Lichtenstein and Andy Warhol are well represented, alongside Picasso.

It's thumbs up for modern art

◆
NÆSTVED
Try to visit Næstved at noon when the cavalry squadron of the Royal Guards Hussars ride through the town blowing trumpets.

Næstved is the largest town in South Zealand and is steeped in history. Situated at a fjord and river junction it has easy access to the sea and until the 17th century traded with Norway, Scotland and Germany. The port was later expanded in order to take bigger ships.

Sightseeing
The town grew up round a Benedictine monastery, founded in 1135, in an attractive riverside setting. Since the Reformation this building has served as a boarding school called **Herlufsholm**, after its founder, Herluf Trolle. The adjoining red-brick church was restored and enlarged in the 13th century. Inside is an ivory crucifix from the same date, an ornate altar, and the splendid sarcophagus of the founder.

Medieval Næstved is about 2 miles (3km) south of the monastery, with cobbled streets and low, half-timbered houses huddled round the restored Gothic **Skt Peders Kirke** (St Peter's Church), the largest in Denmark. It has vaulted ceilings, a fresco of King Valdemar Atterdag (1340–75) and medieval choir stalls. Yet remarkably a third medieval church still stands – **Skt Mortens** (St Martin's), with a large and wonderfully carved altarpiece. This church adjoins one of the many half-timbered houses, **Apostelhuset**, with early religious carvings. Close by a row of medieval brick houses (Boderne) is now part of the **Næstved Museum**, displaying some of the glass and ceramics for which the town is renowned. Another part of the museum, in the Helligåndshuset (House of the Holy Spirit) exhibits medieval sculptures.

You can visit the old **Kähler Ceramic Works** on weekday mornings, and the world-famous **Holmegaards Glasværker** (Glassworks) at Fensmark.

Accommodation and Restaurants

Hotel Vinhuset, 200 years old with a vaulted cellar, but modernised and comfortable, is central (tel: 53 72 08 07). **Menstrup Kro** is just as old, but about 8 miles (13km) west of Næstved, with an indoor pool and a good restaurant (tel: 53 74 30 03). **Herlufsholmskovens** (tel: 53 72 74 43), in the woods north of town, provides traditional Danish food. In Næstved, **Det Røde Pakhus** on Riddergåde and **Rådhuskroen** on Skomagerrækken, are both reliable restaurants.

Excursions from Næstved

On a small island about 5 miles (8km) southwest of Næstved lies **Gavnø**, an 18th-century house and garden built on the site of a former convent. The rococo-style house has an outstanding collection of pictures by Danish and foreign artists, fine 18th- and 19th-century examples of European furniture, and a small but colourful former convent chapel. In the extensive and well-maintained grounds is a rose garden. There are also collections of fire engines and tropical butterflies. About 10 miles (16km) northeast of Næstved is **Gisselfeld**, a 16th-century red-brick Renaissance castle in a breathtaking lakeside setting. The swans here inspired Hans Christian Andersen to write his fairy tale *The Ugly Duckling*. The castle is not open, but the large English-style wooded park is.

◆◆◆
ROSKILDE ✓

The role played by Roskilde in Danish history is a result of its strategic position at the end of the fjord, which led to it becoming a Viking stronghold. Bishop Absalon's cathedral was established in the 12th century and it became a religious focus for the region and Denmark's capital city until 1400. The town enjoyed prosperity and power at this period. Even after the court moved to Copenhagen, all Danish monarchs have been buried here since the 15th century. After the Reformation (1536) the town declined, and did not revive until the railway came in 1847 from Copenhagen. Roskilde is still a commercial centre, and each summer hosts one of Europe's biggest rock festivals.

Sightseeing

The **Domkirken** (the Cathedral) was built on the site of Harald Bluetooth's first wooden church (about 960). Bishop Absalon's cathedral was established in 1170, a red-brick building in Romanesque and Gothic styles. Its towers and green copper spires were added at a later date. The cathedral's interior is light and fairly plain, but enriched by the fine gilded altar screen and a pulpit of marble and alabaster.

Good-value Tourist Ticket
Your **Copenhagen Card** can be used for Roskilde (see page 26). A **Roskilde Card**, valid for a year, gives half-price entry to all sights in town.

More impressive than the architecture are the 38 **royal tombs**, from Queen Margrete (who died in 1412) to the father of the present queen, Frederik IX (who died in 1972), and whose grave is marked by a granite slab outside the cathedral. The other royal remains are inside chapels, in sarcophagi which display various degrees of richness – marble, silver and bronze. Particularly interesting are the large neo-classical chapel of Frederik V, the decorated and vaulted chapel of Christian IV, and that of Christian I, where a granite pillar is marked with the height of various kings, including Peter the Great. Leave time to see the **Cathedral Museum** in the Great Hall above the Chapel of the Magi.

The former **Palæsamlingerne** (Bishop's Palace), linked to the cathedral by an archway, has a collection of furniture and paintings from 18th- and 19th-century merchants' homes. The **Brødrene Lützhøfts Købmandsgård** (Lützhoft Brothers' General Store) is an unusual museum of the 1920s, cluttered with goods as varied as rope, herrings, clogs and sugarloaves, all for sale. One of the greatest finds of recent years is housed in the **Vikingeskibshallen** (Viking Ship Museum), Strandengen, at the edge of the fjord.

The museum itself is a beautiful modern structure, one side of glass almost bringing the fjord into the building. It displays the black remains of five Viking sailing ships which were sunk

across the narrow neck of the fjord in about AD 1000 to prevent the enemy's fleets from attacking the town.

The ships were discovered in 1957 and raised in 1962; since then the vessels have undergone a lengthy process of conservation and reconstruction, with the missing parts now indicated in metal. MS *Sagafjord* runs boat trips on Roskilde Fjord.

Accommodation

Hotel Prindsen, in the centre of town, is an elegant and comfortable hotel (tel: 42 35 80 10) with a good restaurant.

Svogerslev Kro (tel: 46 38 30 05) is 2½ miles (4km) west of Roskilde, a lovely thatched building in extensive grounds.

Gershøj Kro (tel: 47 52 80 41) is in a small fishing village on the north side of the fjord. It specialises in eel dishes.

Restaurants

Two central and historic eating places, both with gardens, are **Rådhuskælderen** (tel: 42 36 01 00) with vaulted cellars and **Club 42** (tel: 42 35 17 64), cosy yet lively, in the pedestrian area of the town.

Excursions from Roskilde

Ledreborg Slot og Park (Ledreborg Castle and Park) is an 18th-century Versailles-style palace, set in a terraced park, 6 miles (10km) west of Roskilde.

It has been the home of the Holstein–Ledreborg family since 1739, and the fine rooms contain excellent paintings. Chandeliers, tapestries and gilded furniture abound; there is a beautiful baroque chapel and an old kitchen. The castle gives spectacular views over the valley and you can stroll round the tree-filled park.

Lejre Forsøgsenter (Research Centre) is a delightful place set in wooded hills about 6 miles (10km) west of Roskilde where history has really been brought to life. An Iron Age village, with farms, ancient breeds of animals, and even a Sacrificial Bog has been re-created. In another part of the site, you can inspect Danish agriculture as it was 150 years ago, by visiting reconstructed farm cottages, surrounded by gardens and grazing livestock. In summer, activities such as weaving and pottery take place in experimental workshops. Children can try making Iron Age biscuits.

◆◆◆
RUNGSTED

Fans of *Out of Africa*, the creation of novelist Karen Blixen (alias Isak Dinesen), should not fail to visit Rungstedlund, the childhood home to which she returned from Africa in 1931, after the collapse of her farming venture. She lived here until her death in 1962 and now this large, gracious house, on the coast between Copenhagen and Helsingør, is the **Karen Blixen Museum**.

The former stables house an evocative display of photographs of the author, from her Danish childhood to a dignified old age, often in the company of the famous, and including her life in Africa.

She wrote in English, rewriting her work in Danish for publication, and many of her manuscripts and letters home are on display, as well as a library of her works.

Guided tours (overshoes compulsory) include the rooms where Karen Blixen lived and wrote. They are unchanged since her death: the cosy green study, overlooking the garden; the comfortable drawing room; the writing room, with its fine view of the harbour and its Masai spears and other souvenirs she brought back from Africa.

Karen Blixen was also a talented artist, and a small collection of her works, painted in Africa and Denmark, may be seen.

She preserved the 40-acre (16ha) park as a bird sanctuary, and she was laid to rest beneath a simple stone slab under a beech tree situated in the northwest corner.

◆
VORDINGBORG

Vordingborg, in the southwest of Zealand, is linked to the island of Falster by a bridge. Most of the town is modern, but the **Gåsetårnet** (Goose Tower), which stands on a grassy hill, is the only survivor of four corner towers of the curtain wall which surrounded a 12th-century castle (later demolished). Valdemar Atterdag decreed that a gilded goose should crown the tower, to mock the towns of the Hanseatic League.

Climb the Goose Tower for some fine views, and take a walk along the walls.

The former cavalry barracks is now the **South Zealand Museum** which has exhibits from the Stone Age and collections of tools and textiles. There is a small **Botanical Garden** near by.

Accommodation and Restaurants

Hotel Kong Valdemar at Algåde 101 (tel: 53 77 00 95) is near the Goose Tower and **Udby Kro** (tel: 53 78 10 02), one of Denmark's oldest inns, about 6 miles (10km) north at Lundby, offers a good choice of food in a pleasant setting.

NORTH ZEALAND COAST

The sandy beaches of the north coast provide an easy summer escape from Copenhagen.

The unusual church at Kalundborg

Without a car, you can get to the resorts by train, then it's about 15 minutes walk to the sea.

WHAT TO SEE

◆
GILLELEJE

Gilleleje is Zealand's northernmost point, a popular resort and the largest fishing port in Zealand. Fish auctions are held here on weekdays. The **Gilleleje Museet** is an old schoolhouse and has reminders of this land's earliest settlers. There is also the **Gilleleje Museums Skibshal** (Fishing Museum).

A footpath runs along the top of the dunes to **Gilbjerg Hoved** from where there is a spectacular view and a memorial to the philosopher Søren Kierkegaard.

NORTH ZEALAND COAST

The **Nakkehoved Øster Fyr** lighthouse was built in 1772, and is the only preserved coal-fired lighthouse in the world. Inland, Gilleleje has many old half-timbered, thatched houses, two museums, and a simple 16th-century church.

Accommodation and Restaurants

The pleasant **Hotel Strand** is Gilleleje's only hotel and overlooks the sea (tel: 48 30 05 12). **Gilleleje Havn** is a fish restaurant by the harbour and **Fyrkroen**, near the lighthouse at Nakkehoved, serves cold table lunches at weekends.

◆◆
HORNBÆK

Hornbaek is another former fishing village which is now a popular summer resort, its beaches and dunes backed by thick woods, planted 200 years ago to provide protection from gales. Passages wind between the old red and yellow houses, leading up to the 18th-century sailors' church with its collection of model ships.

Accommodation and Restaurants

Hotel Trouville (tel: 42 20 22 00) is close to the forest and beach and has an indoor pool. **Søstrene Olsen** (tel: 42 20 05 50) is a seafood restaurant close to the harbour.

◆
TISVILDELEJE

Tisvildeleje is an attractive and often crowded resort on the north coast, with white-sand beaches. South of the village is **Tisvilde Hegn**, a forest of gnarled trees planted in the last century to stabilise the drifting sand. There are good coastal walks and views across to Sweden.

Accommodation

Tisvildeleje Strandhotel (tel: 42 30 71 19) is comfortable.

ZEALAND'S ISLANDS

The three large, green and
rather flat islands off the south
coast of Zealand – Falster,
Lolland and Møn – are within
easy reach of Copenhagen.

WHAT TO SEE

FALSTER
Falster has a few good beaches
on the east coast: one of the
most popular is **Marielyst**.
The main town, **Nykøbing F**, is
a lively place with pavement
cafés, street theatre and a
mini-zoo (free) in **Folkeparken**.
Of several medieval buildings,
the most notable is the
half-timbered **Czarens Hus**
(Tsar's House), named after
Peter the Great's visit. It is now
home to the **Museet Falsters
Minder** (Memorial Museum),
which displays local finds. The
Middelaldercentret takes a
new angle on life in the Middle
Ages by examining its
technology and weaponry;
knights give jousting displays.
Energetic visitors can climb the
Vandtårn (water tower) in
Hollands Gård.

LOLLAND
Lolland is Denmark's third
largest island, completely flat
apart from some hills in the
northwest, and fertile,
producing large quantities of
sugar beet. The island is
scattered with big country
estates, some of which are open
to the public, and there are
some excellent beaches,
particularly around **Kramnitse**.

Sightseeing
The largest town is **Nakskov**,
home of Denmark's biggest
sugar refinery. Between the
market square, with its
17th-century pharmacy, and the
harbour, is a picturesque area
of narrow lanes with old shops.
The tall spire of **Skt Nikolai
Kirke** (St Nicholas Church)
dominates the town – a Swedish
cannonball, fired in 1659, is
lodged in the chancel arch.
Near by is **Den Gamle Smedie**
(the old smithy) where you can
watch horses being shod.
Near Pederstrup is the
Reventlow-museet, set in an
English-style park. This classical
building was the family home of
C D F Reventlow (1748–1827),
famous for his role in liberating
the peasants and educational
reforms.
Maribo is a delightful town with
cobbled streets, pastel-coloured
cottages and a red-brick
cathedral by a lake. **Maribo
Domkirke** (Cathedral) was
formerly the abbey church,
founded in 1416 and restored in
the last century. Its white
rib-vaulted interior sets off the
painted Renaissance pulpit and
ornate gold altar. The remains of
a convent built at the same time
including pillar bases, once part
of the nuns' cloister and
refectory, stand between the
cathedral and lake.
At **Knuthenborg Safari Park**, in
the grounds of an old manor
house, 900 species of animals
and birds, including giraffes,
emus and rhinos, graze
amongst the chewed-off tree
trunks. As well as the animals,
there is **Småland** (Miniworld), a
children's amusement park.

Accommodation

In Maribo, **Ebsens Hotel** (tel: 53 88 10 44) is central and comfortable, while the large **Hotel Hvide Hus** (tel: 53 88 10 11) overlooks the lakes. **Hotel Harmonien** at Nakskov (tel: 53 92 21 00) is central and suitable for families. **Hotel og Restaurant Skovridergaarden** (tel: 53 92 03 55) is an old country inn.

Restaurants

In Maribo, **Bangs Have** (tel: 53 88 19 11) overlooks the harbour, while **Café Maribo**, at Vestergade 6B, offers tasty *smørrebrøds*. In Nakskov, try **Vinkælderen** (Axeltorv 9), for fish dishes. In Nykøbing, you can dine in panelled splendour at **Czarens Hus**, Langgade 2.

Excursions from Lolland

Near Nysted, the 12th-century **Aalholm Slot** (Castle) is one of the oldest inhabited castles in the country and has finely furnished rooms, a torture chamber and a family ghost. In the grounds is the **Automobilmuseum** (Car Museum), one of Denmark's largest collections of veteran cars. A steam train runs from here to the beach. Another steam train, the **Museumsbanen**, chugs across Lolland, from Bandholm to Maribo on summer weekends. You can explore the **Maribo Lakes** by boat or walk round them on marked trails. Boats sail from Kragenæs to the nearby islands of Fejø and Femø and from Bandholm to the island of Askø, while the post boat sails to little islands in Nakskov Fjord.

MØN

This is the prettiest, the most rural and the least accessible of the three islands. The dramatic chalk cliffs on the east coast (**Møns Klint**) stretch for 5 miles (8km). **Klintholm Havn**, a small fishing village, and **Liselund Manor**, built in the 18th century, are both worth visiting. Liselund has a pleasant park with three summer-houses – Hans Christian Andersen is said to have written *The Tinderbox* in one of them.

Neolithic people inhabited Møn, and long barrows (including **Kong Askers Høj**) and Bronze Age tombs are scattered around the island. So are whitewashed village churches, with medieval frescoes; **Fanefjord**, **Keldby**, and **Elmelunde** are the best. **Stege** is the main town, with preserved medieval ramparts, and the **Møn Museum** displays local finds.

The **Ulvshale peninsula** is a nature reserve and its sandy beaches are amongst the finest in Denmark. From here, visit the tiny island of **Nyord** where farms have barely changed in 300 years.

Accommodation

You can stay in style at **Liselund Slot** (tel: 55 81 20 81), near the manor house, with a good restaurant. Much cheaper and in Stege itself is **Pension Elmehøj** (tel: 55 81 35 35) with good sea views; half board is possible. There are several bed and breakfast places on Møn and it is possible to rent summer cottages.

Peace and Quiet

Wildlife and Countryside in Denmark by Paul Sterry

As a general rule, the more geographical variety a country has, the more diverse its plant and animal life, and hence the greater its natural history interest. With this in mind, Denmark might seem a rather unpromising destination since it is uniformly low-lying (most of the land being less than 400 feet (120m) above sea level) and has little natural habitat left. But, in fact, Denmark has a lot to offer the visitor interested in natural history, especially one whose interests also embrace geology and archaeology.

In geographical terms, Denmark is fragmented: in addition to its main land mass (the Jutland peninsula), there are more than 400 islands. This means that the coastline is extensive.

The entire landscape, given its basic 'shape' by the effects of glaciation, has been heavily modified by humans. Across the country, there are archaeological remains that remind visitors of the long settlement of Denmark, and examples of modern farming practices are reminders of contemporary land use – nearly three-quarters of the land is agricultural. However, there are still some remnant areas of natural habitats – dunes, freshwater marshes, heaths and forests – and, fortunately, much of Denmark's wildlife is very adaptable, many birds, for example, living in comparative harmony with the altered landscape.

A red-backed shrike, one of many woodland species to be seen here

PEACE AND QUIET

Not surprisingly, visiting birdwatchers will find most interest in the coastal birds. Waders, gulls, terns, ducks and geese are abundant, although the species to be seen vary throughout the year. Some are summer visitors while others are year-round residents. Spring and autumn are particularly rewarding because hundreds of thousands of other species pass through on migration. Interesting plant life is more or less confined to coastal districts and small areas of natural or semi-natural habitat protected by reserve status and often with restricted access.

In and Around Copenhagen

Although Copenhagen is a bustling modern city, it has several havens of tranquility with a natural history interest. Birdwatchers will find that small, wooded parks have many interesting species – mainly in spring and summer – and parkland lakes, canals and waterfronts have birds throughout the year. Woodland birds may include barred warblers and thrush nightingales. The latter are rather secretive, but visitors cannot fail to miss their loud song, often sung after dark. Lakes and waterways have grebes, ducks, geese and terns in the summer months. In winter, many birds leave and fly south, to be replaced by other, more hardy species. Look for several species of gulls as well as lots of ducks. One of the more regularly encountered is the smew. This small diving

duck has mostly white plumage in the male, and grey plumage, with a chestnut head, in the female. They are often found on surprisingly small areas of water.

Although almost any suitable looking area of woodland, seashore or lake is worth exploring, some of the better birdwatching spots in and around Copenhagen are as follows:

Fredriksberg Have – woodland and formal gardens
Utterslev Mose – woods and freshwater in a parkland setting
Amager – an island to the south of Copenhagen.

Look for coastal birds in and around the pretty little fishing village of Dragør and woodland birds in Kongelunden.

Woodland Birds

Spring is the best time of year to look for woodland birds in Denmark. Many of the breeding species are summer migrants, flying south to their wintering grounds in August and September.

Several species of warblers can be seen, the smallest being the willow warbler, whose song is a delightful, descending trill, and the chiffchaff, whose song is exactly like its name. Icterine warblers and barred warblers are also widespread, the latter often being found in close proximity to red-backed shrikes in areas of scrub vegetation. Nuthatches and several species of tits are year-round residents, as is Denmark's most distinctive bird, the crow-sized black woodpecker.

Calm water on Roskilde Fjord

Rands Fjord Nature Park

At one time this fjord was midway between Vejle and Fredericia on Jutland's east coast, connected with the sea, but it became landlocked in comparatively recent times and is now freshwater in nature. To reach the park, drive southeast from Vejle. Roughly 4 miles (6km) beyond Børkop, the road crosses the eastern edge of the park, just before you reach the village of Egeskov. Much of the area can be seen by exploring the minor roads running along the northern edge of the park – between Overhøl, Nebbegård and Østerskov – and to the south between Egeskov and Østerskov.

The fjord lake is important as a stopping-off point for migrant waders and wildfowl, while the marshes and reed-beds harbour breeding birds such as reed warblers and bearded tits.

North Zealand

Using Copenhagen as a base, there are several excellent wildlife sites within easy reach of the city for those visitors with a car:

Nekselø Nature Reserve is a small island sited on the northwest coast of Zealand, roughly 75 miles (120km) west of Copenhagen. Drive west from the city to Jyderup and then northwest to Havnsø, from where you can take a boat to the island. Visitors will find a mixture of meadows, valleys and lakes here. Meadow flowers are good in the spring and wetland birds breed here.

Roskilde Fjord is a beautiful fjord surrounded by attractive countryside, roughly 19 miles (30km) west of Copenhagen. Three parts of the southern end of the fjord have been designated Landscape Protection Areas. Roads run along both the eastern and western shores from Roskilde to Frederikssund and through Skibby and Skuldelev respectively. Along the shores, visitors will find freshwater lakes, beech woodlands and meadows, full of breeding birds in summer and migrant and wintering wildfowl and waders at other times of the year.

PEACE AND QUIET

Hillerød lies 19 miles (30km) northwest of Copenhagen and is a central point for several sites of natural history interest. Just to the north of the town is the forest of Gribskov, one of Denmark's largest. The trees are a mixture of beech and pine. Waymarked walks and trails allow easy access, and visitors can look for woodland birds such as icterine warblers, nuthatches, pied flycatchers, buzzards and honey-buzzards. One of the specialities of the area is the black woodpecker. On the eastern edge of the forest and between Hillerød and the town of Helsingør is a lake known as **Esrum Sø**. The area is a nature reserve, mainly because of its importance to wintering wildfowl, and footpaths allow for easy exploration. South of Hillerød is **Store Dyrehave** (the Great Deer Park), an area of open, park woodland.

Farum Nature Park is less than 12 miles (20km) from the outskirts of Copenhagen, northwest of the city. A network of footpaths allows visitors to explore the marshy ground and the three lakes within the park. Wetland birds and marsh flowers can be seen.

Southern Zealand and Adjacent Islands

As you travel south from Copenhagen, the scenery becomes increasingly rural. There are several areas of particular interest to the visitor: **Tystrup Nature Park** lies between Ringsted and Fuglebjerg in southwest Zealand. Lakes, marshes, woodland and meadows make up this reserve, which is good for breeding and wintering wildfowl and waterbirds.

Høje Møn Nature Park occupies the eastern tip of Møn, and has interesting chalk cliffs. **Ulvshale Nature Park**, the oldest in Denmark, is on the northwestern tip of Møn and has a varied mix of heathland (juniper and heather), coastal meadow and a rare example of primeval forest.

Gedser, on the island of Falster, is the southernmost point of Denmark. Migrant birds are often concentrated here in spring, but more especially in autumn. Look for birds of prey, including sparrowhawks and honey-buzzards.

Farmland Birds

Over the centuries, good use has been made of Denmark's lowland soils, and farmland is the country's most widespread habitat. Although wildlife is increasingly being edged out of the picture, a good many species are adaptable and live alongside people.

Arable fields harbour such hardy birds as rooks, pheasants and grey partridges while, near the coast, flocks of geese and ducks can sometimes be seen in autumn and winter.

Where meadows are left for haymaking, there is usually a rich and colourful flora. Small mammals abound, and predators such as kestrels and buzzards take advantage of their numbers.

Practical

This section includes information on food, drink, shopping, accommodation, nightlife, tight budget, special events etc.

FOOD AND DRINK

There is little regional variation in Danish food and though it is not cheap, the quality is consistently high.

As Denmark is surrounded by the sea, it is not surprising that **fish**, such as herring, plaice, salmon and shellfish feature widely on menus. Traditional fish dishes include *gravad laks* (salmon marinated in dill, served with a sweet mustard dressing), *jomfruhummer* (Norwegian crayfish), and *rødspættefilet remoulade* (fillet of plaice with remoulade sauce). Roe (*rogn*) and eel (*ål*) also feature frequently.

The choice of **meat** is usually limited to pork, beef and veal. British visitors will be surprised not to find any bacon (the Danes export it all). Try *frikadeller* (pork meatballs served with a thick gravy), *fransk bøf* (fillet steak with parsley butter and chips), *mørbradbøf* (pork tenderloin with mushroom sauce) and *skipperlabskovs* (thick beef stew). *Biksemad* consists of meat, potatoes and fried onion,

and *medisterpølse* is a spiced pork sausage.

Popular **puddings** include *pandekager* (pancakes), *æblekage* (a type of apple cake) and *rødgrød* (red berry jelly), always generously laced with *fløde* (cream) or *flødeskum* (whipped cream). A huge range of *is* (ice cream) is sold. Specific to Denmark is *smørrebrød* (open sandwiches) – a slice of *rugbrød* (rye bread) with a generous topping of, perhaps, roast beef or pork, liver pâté, shrimps in mayonnaise, egg or cheese, always artistically decorated with pickles, lemon or salad stuff. *Koldt bord* (cold table) is a huge help-yourself buffet – once widely available, but now only served at Copenhagen station and a few large hotels. It features both cold food (herring, salads, shellfish, smoked fish, meats) and hot dishes (soup, vegetables, stew), as well as cheese and desserts – all temptingly displayed. But resist the temptation to heap all the food on your plate together – follow local custom and take just a few items, starting with herring.

FOOD AND DRINK

Each time you come back for more food, take a clean plate.

Drink

Beer is very popular, and produced by the country's two main breweries, Carlsberg and Tuborg. It is sold mainly in pubs and bars, as well as in *bodegas* and cafés which serve wine too (imported and therefore expensive). Generally, cafés open in the morning, pubs may open from noon.

The drinking laws are less severe than in the rest of Scandinavia and alcohol can be bought in supermarkets. Most Danish beer is *pilsner* (lager), sold in 0.75-litre bottles. *Lys pilsner* is the lightest; *fadøl* (draught lager) is stronger and sold in 0.5-litre sizes; *luxøl* (*Eksport* or *Guldøl* brands) is stronger still, and *elefantøl* is a very strong special beer.

The Danes produce their own potato-based **schnapps** called *akvavit*, which may be flavoured with dill or caraway and is typically drunk ice-cold in a single gulp.

Tea (*the*) and coffee (*kaffe*) are widely available. Coffee is served black, often in a jug to give two cups, with separate cream or milk. Tap water (*vand*) is safe to drink throughout Denmark.

Meals and Mealtimes

Hotel breakfasts (*morgenmad*) are usually large, help-yourself affairs to set you up for the day. They may include fruit juice, cereals, milk, yogurt, fruit, cheese, cold meats, liver pâté, bread, rolls, Danish pastries, jam and tea or coffee.

Lunch (*frokost*) usually served from noon–14.00hrs can be anything from a snack to a full meal. Many eating places offer lunchtime bargains in the form of a *tilbud* (special offer), which is a reduced price main course or a *dagen's ret* (dish of the day), a fixed-price main course with extras – starter, pudding, or a drink. These offers may only be available for a limited time, perhaps just at lunchtime, and the same meal will cost more in the evening.

Evening meals (*aftensmad*), usually start early – running from about 17.30 to 20.30hrs, though you can dine until 22.00hrs in larger towns.

Eating Out

Restaurant meals are attractively presented: the portions are generous and there is frequently a children's menu (*børnemenu*) or children's dishes (*børneretter*). The restaurants recommended in this book serve predominantly Danish food. You will also find many ethnic and fast food restaurants, especially in the cities, and vegetarians and diabetics are well catered for. Bistros, *bodegas* and cafés sell light, inexpensive meals and drinks, and self-service cafeterias are often located in supermarkets and department stores. *Konditorier* specialise in creamy pastries, cakes and drinks, while grillbars and *fiskerestauranter* (fish restaurants) are self-explanatory. *Pølsevogn* are kiosks, often found in town squares, selling fast food such as sausages and hamburgers.

Kros (inns), hotels and motels generally have a restaurant and while pubs concentrate on beer, they also sell snacks.

DSB restaurants at railway stations are reliably good and usually offer a set three-course meal, fast food and special children's dishes.

Food Shops

Denmark is well supplied with supermarkets and there are several chains (Irma, Netto, Kvickly) where you can easily buy picnic food – pâté, cold meats, cheese, prepared salads (often with egg or fish) and yogurts. Fishmongers also sell salads and snacks. *Bageri* (bakers' shops) are open on Sunday mornings.

SHOPPING

Traffic-free pedestrian zones make shopping a very pleasant experience in Denmark. Large shopping malls are the pride of Aalborg, Esbjerg and Roskilde. Denmark is well known for its excellent design, and goods on sale are always attractively displayed, of a high quality and rather expensive. Its beautiful glass, porcelain and silverware are world-famous. Jewellery, often set with semi-precious stones, or items made from amber washed ashore on Danish beaches make very acceptable gifts. Furniture is a bulky purchase, but can be shipped. As the country is small, most common goods are available everywhere, but larger towns naturally offer a greater choice. There are few department stores; the best and most famous is Illum in Copenhagen. Fashion is a high export earner, and designer names are widely flaunted. Furs – if you can bring yourself to wear them – leather goods and heavy knitted sweaters can be good value. In summer, many clothes and shoe shops put racks outside with special offers (*tilbud*) and sales are a source of bargains.

Danes have deft fingers and many shops sell a wide range of wool, knitting patterns and needlecraft supplies. Ready-made cushion covers and wall-hangings make good presents. Table decorations, such as candle-holders and candles, on sale with matching paper napkins, are fun to buy.

Danish cuisine is rich and varied

Value Added Tax

VAT (called MOMS in Danish) is high, but you can save by going to one of 2,900 shops displaying a Europe Tax-free Shopping logo. You have to spend a minimum amount in the same shop before you are entitled to a refund. This scheme is only available to residents outside EU or Nordic countries. To obtain a refund you must keep copies of your tax-free receipt(s), which must be stamped at the customs point when you leave Denmark. Kastrup Airport. You are then entitled to a cash refund in most currencies. Alternatively, send your stamped receipt(s) to **Europe Tax-free Shopping Denmark**, Kastruplundgåde 22.1, DK-2770 Kastrup, and you will eventually be reimbursed; a small administrative charge is made.

ACCOMMODATION

Hotels

Denmark offers a wide choice of places to stay, from expensive hotels to campsites. Several hotel chains operate in Denmark and some issue vouchers offering discounts at certain times of the year. **Dan**

Accommodation Guides
Denmark is produced by the Danish Tourist Board, and describes all accommodation. *Hotels* and *Camping/Youth and Family Hostels* give addresses, telephone numbers, prices and facilities. The *Camping* list also notes where caravans and tents can be hired. (See page 112.)

Hotels offer a Scandinavian Bonus Pass (Inter Dan Hotel, Langdraget 110, DK-2820 Gilleleje) and **Best Western Hotels** and **Scandic Hotels** also offer discounts. Addresses from the publication *Hotels* (see Box). Inn cheques (*krocheck*) are valid at about 90 independent inns which have formed a group and offer discounts from 10 to 25 per cent – write to **Dansk Kroferie**, Vejlevej 16, DK-8700 Horsens. Strangely enough, the cost of some accommodation can be lower during the peak holiday months (June to August), particularly at hotels which normally cater for the business fraternity. Several of the more expensive hotels in Copenhagen also reduce their prices at weekends, Christmas and Easter.

Hotels are not graded, but are of a uniformly high standard and very clean. At the top end of the market are a few manor houses, elegant mansions often centuries old, which offer modern standards of accommodation and very good meals too. At the other end of the price scale are seamen's hotels, located at many ports (no longer only for sailors) which can be fairly basic, and mission hotels, which serve no alcohol.

Self-catering

Many Danes own a summer house on the coast, on an island or tucked away in the country, which they let during the summer. They may be simple structures of wood, brick or stone, and some are thatched. Holiday companies rent out

summer cottages too, fully furnished and equipped except for towels and bed linen. Summer houses sleep from two to eight people and range from the fairly basic, to those with shower and refrigerator, to luxury with sauna and indoor swimming pool. Prices depend on the month – May and September are the cheapest. This type of accommodation is best booked in advance from tourist offices or from special booking agents, listed in the Danish Tourist Board's annual brochure *Denmark*.

Another variation is to stay at one of the **holiday centres** which provide little houses or apartments, usually on the coast. These sleep from two to eight people and are likely to have television and a washing machine. Again, you supply your own towels and linen. Some apartments have kitchens, but there is a café and a restaurant on site. The centres offer many activities, usually including a swimming pool, table tennis, billiards, sauna and a play area for children.

One company, Dansk Folkeferie, Gammel Kongevej 33, DK-1610, Copenhagen V, runs 11 centres. More information from same sources as above.

Farmhouse Holidays

This kind of accommodation is very popular and offers two alternatives: you can stay in the farmhouse and eat with the family (either just breakfast, or supper too), or you can stay in a separate self-catering cottage or flat. Write to: Danish Farm Holidays, Søndergade 26,

It is possible to rent cottages, or you might consider a home-swap

DK-8700, Horsens; or to Landsforeningen for Landboturisme, Lerbakken 7, DK-8410, Rønde.

Private Accommodation

You can stay in Danish homes – book through a local tourist office, at the tourist board's accommodation office in Copenhagen, or through **Host and Guest Service**, 27 Effie Road, London SW6 1EN (tel: 0171-736 5340). A free **bed and breakfast** catalogue is available from Dansk BoligBytte, PO Box 53, DK-2900, Hellerup and from local tourist offices.

Home Exchange

Another good idea for families is to swap homes, complete with the toys and bicycles. More information from **HomeLink International**, (tel: 01344-842642. (Remember Danish school holidays are from late June until early August).

Youth Hostels

Youth and Family Hostels (Danmarks Vandrerhjem) – 110 of them – are dotted all over Denmark in town and country, in various types of buildings and represent very good value for money. The sleeping arrangements range from two beds to dormitories, but most are four or six-bedded, called family rooms, complete with shower and toilet.

A big breakfast is always available but evening meals depend on the whim of the warden. However, most hostels have a kitchen, usually with fridge, crockery and saucepans where you can cook your own food (take matches in case there is only gas).

For people travelling alone, especially cyclists, hostels are ideal and cost about a quarter, or less, of the price for one person using a two-bedded hotel room. It is always best to book in advance. In high season, you cannot stay longer than three nights in the same hostel. Join the Youth Hostels Association in your own country before you set off, and buy a sheet sleeping bag – otherwise you will have to hire one each night. In Denmark, the address is **Landsforeningen Danmarks Vandrerhjem**, Vesterbrogade 39, DK-1620, Copenhagen V. They publish an English edition of their hostels guide, with photos and maps. A list of hostels is also available from the Danish Tourist Board. These days it is not necessary to arrive on foot or by cycle; you can drive to a youth hostel – and you can be *any* age.

CULTURE, ENTERTAINMENT AND NIGHTLIFE

Denmark is a sophisticated country, and this is evident in its approach to culture. Civic pride also plays its part in attracting visitors, with well-maintained buildings and gardens, statues of local worthies or modern sculptures and fountains placed at strategic points. There is competition between local museums for the most lively presentation of their town's history, which often goes far back to prehistoric times. Throughout Denmark old buildings are being carefully restored, and there are a number of reconstructed villages. Much importance is placed on modern art, and numerous galleries, often privately owned, are open to the public.

The Danes love music, and classical concerts are performed in museums, manor houses and churches, as well as in large city concert halls.

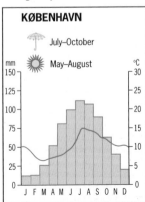

KØBENHAVN

July–October

May–August

enjoy – such as coffees, cakes, ice creams and drinks – may cost more than at home. The two cheapest ways of visiting Denmark are bringing your car (full) and self-catering, or cycling round and staying at youth hostels. It is possible to stay at youth hostels and use public transport, but careful planning is essential because some hostels are a long way from the nearest public transport.

Budget Tips
- Plan your trip to coincide with discount air fares.
- If you are taking your car, look for bargain fares offered by Scandinavian Seaways.
- If planning to hire a car, it is often cheaper to book in advance in your own country.
- If you are self-catering, bring all the basics with you.
- Supermarkets in towns offer best-value food shopping, but look also at fruit and vegetable stalls in street markets.
- If eating out, bistros and cafés sell light, inexpensive meals, and there are self-service cafeterias, often located in supermarkets and department stores; have your main meal at lunchtime, when set-price meals and other bargains are often available (see page 96).
- If you like the occasional drink, bring in the maximum amount of alcohol permitted for your own consumption.
- Travel cards issued by certain towns can be money savers.
- Family groups looking for accommodation should ask about the availability of family rooms (see also **Accommodation**, page 98).

SPECIAL EVENTS

It would seem that there is little time for work in Denmark in summer with all that is going on – town and music festivals, markets and fairs, concerts, sporting events, exhibitions and anniversary celebrations. Many towns hold weekly jazz concerts and some churches and castles, such as Spøttrup (Balling) and Kolding have classical music concerts. Trotting races are held in Copenhagen, Århus and some other towns, and regattas and angling competitions take place everywhere. Tilting contests and animal fairs are regularly held in South Jutland, and Midsummer's Eve (23 June) is celebrated throughout Denmark with bonfires and local entertainment.

The Danish Tourist Board publishes a comprehensive booklet, *Coming Events*, twice a year. This lists activities between April and September, and from October to March. A separate leaflet, *Danish Music Festivals*, is produced by the Danish Music Information Centre (Gråbrødertorv 16, DK-1154, Copenhagen K). A selection of events is given below; most last for a day or weekend unless otherwise stated:

April
Løgumkloster: Spring Fair
Viborg: Horse and Junk Fair

May
Assens: Harbour Festival
Copenhagen: Carnival
Middelfart: Little Belt Jazz
   Festival

Nyborg: Whitsun Fair
Nykøbing Mors: Pearl Festival
Ribe: Tulip Festival
Aalborg: Festival (one week)

June

Fåborg: Festival
Frederikssund: Viking Festival
(two weeks)
Karrebæksminde: Jazz Festival
Odense: Summer Festival (until
August)
Odense: Harbour Festival
Ringe: Midtfyns (Central Funen
Festival – rock and folk music)
Roskilde: Agricultural Show
Roskilde: Festival (rock music,
theatre, fair)
Silkeborg: Riverboat Jazz
Festival
Skagen: Festival (folk and rock)
Sønderborg: Shooting
Festival
Aalborg: Jazz Festival
Egeskov: Summer Festival

July

Bornholm: Herring Festival
(four days)
Bornholm: Music Festival (until
first week September)
Copenhagen: Summer Festival
(classical music – until
mid-August)
Copenhagen: Jazz Festival (one
week)
Fredericia: Jazz Festival
Maribo: Jazz Festival
Samsø : Festival (jazz and folk)
Skørping and Aalborg: Rebild
Festival (4 July)
Sønderborg: Tilting Festival
Ærø: Grolle Festival
Åbenrå: County Tilting Festival
(including Tattoo)
Århus: International Jazz
Festival (one week)
Århus: Viking Moot
Jels: Viking plays

August

Ebeltoft: Festival (music)
Esbjerg: North Sea Days
Fåborg: Harbour Festival
Odense: Film Festival (odd
years only)
Randers: Festival (10 days,
including Regatta)
Roskilde: Viking Fair
Silkeborg: Denmark Grand Prix
(motor races)
Skanderborg: Danmarks
Smukkeste (most beautiful
rock) Festival
Tønder: Folk Music Festival
Viborg: Jazz Festival
Århus: Harbour Festival

September

Højer: Sheep Fair
Næstved: Troll Festival (one
week)
Skanderborg: Tour de
Gudenaa (canoe races)
Århus: Festival and Old-World
Fair (nine days)

SPORT

The Danes are keen on sport,
and tourists can participate in
many activities such as boating
(rowing boats), canoeing,
go-karting, horse riding and
walking. The Danish Tourist
Board can supply you with
information on most of these
sports to help you choose the
most suitable holiday in the best
area (independent or package).

Cycling

The flat landscape makes
Denmark particularly well
suited to cycling and there are
many cycle tracks in and
between towns, as well as an
extensive network of marked
cycle routes. Visitors can bring

their own bike or hire one from a local cycle shop, youth hostel or tourist office at a daily or weekly rate. You must pay a deposit and return the machine to the original hirer.

Bicycles can also be hired at some railway stations and be taken on most trains. The State Railways (DSB) publish a leaflet *Take the Train – Rent a Bike* which gives information about what is available. Cycles can be taken on other forms of transport too, including domestic flights, but not on city buses.

Free Wheeling
A novel scheme introduced in Copenhagen enables visitors to have free use of *bycykler* (city bikes) at several points in the city. You place a coin into the bike and the money is automatically returned when the bike is put back in the stand.

On cycling package holidays you are provided with a bicycle, carriers, route map, accommodation and ferry tickets if needed. You get a discount if you bring your own bike. Many local tourist offices publish maps and routes for cyclists, avoiding main roads. In Jutland particularly, the winds can be strong and you will find journeys from west to east easier (and quicker) than those from east to west!

Dansk Cyklist Forbund
(Danish Cyclists' Federation), Rømersgade 7, DK-1362, Copenhagen, (tel: 33 32 31 21) can give you more information.

Windmills are part of the landscape

Fishing
Denmark is a fisherman's paradise, but you need to bring your own rod and line. For inshore fishing (herring, cod and flatfish) you do not need a licence, and you can fish from harbours or piers and from almost anywhere along the coast. Deep-sea fishing trips with local fishermen can also be arranged.

For fresh-water fishing (trout, eel, salmon), people over 18 years of age need a fishing permit, obtainable from the local tourist office, post office or tackle shop. You will also have to pay a fee, for a day or for a number of hours. 'Put and take' is very popular, where local lakes are specially stocked with fish. Certain restrictions are in force regarding fishing near the mouths of rivers.

You can bring your own maggots, but check with the airline first (the ferries accepts them, sealed) or you can buy them in Denmark.

Package fishing holidays are available, either in hotels or self-catering accommodation, and the fishing licence is included in the price.

Golf

There are over 100 courses in Denmark, most of which have 18 holes. You can hire clubs and a trolley on a daily basis; green fees are higher at weekends. To play on any course you need to show the membership card of a recognised golf club.

The leaflet *Danish Inn Holidays* lists all the courses; some inns offer complimentary or reduced-price green fees. You can buy a golf package holiday which may include green fees.

Sailing

Danish yachting enthusiasts are fortunate that their country is composed of so many islands which provide such excellent and varied sailing. The most attractive areas are around Funen, with 100 islands, and the Limfjord area. As well as the numerous harbours, many new marinas have been built. Swedes, Germans and Dutch visitors can coast-hop to

Denmark (having sought radio permission), but sailors from the UK, for example, will have to negotiate the grim North Sea. You can hire a sailing boat, motor yacht or motorised sailing boat from Nordia Boat Charter, Vestre Alle 50, Hammerum, DK-7400, Herning and Dansk Yacht Charter, Dokvej 4, Marina Nord, DK-6000, Kolding, but you will have to show your certificate of competence. Ask to see the boat's safety certificate too. Help with planning your voyage, such as handbooks and charts, is available from Kort-og Matrikelstyrelsen, Kundekontoret Salgssektionen, Rentemestervej 8, DK-2400, Copenhagen NV.

Swimming

Apart from the sea (see **Beaches** in the **Directory**), most towns have a swimming pool and some also have an Aqualand (see pages 103–4). A slightly unusual version is **Søhøjlandet Centre** at Gjern, northwest of Århus, which offers a range of other sports too – riding, squash and tennis.

Windsurfing

Beginners and experts will enjoy the variety of Denmark's coast, with long inlets and protected shores. Experienced windsurfers should try to aim for the northwest coasts of Jutland, Zealand and Funen, and around Møn, Falster, Langeland and Bornholm. Instruction is available at many centres mostly located on the east coasts of Jutland and Zealand; surfboards can also be hired. Maps are published which grade the areas according to difficulty.

Directory

This section contains day-to-day information, including travel, health, documentation and language tips.

Contents

Arriving

By Air
Denmark does not have its own national airline but has a share in **SAS**, the Scandanavian Airlines System, which operates flights to Copenhagen (Kastrup Airport) from about 70 different countries. About 40 airlines have regular services to Copenhagen, including Air UK, British Airways and British Midland.

The Danish carrier **Maersk** (in London, tel: 0171-333 0066), flies to Billund and Copenhagen from London Gatwick. Maersk also flies to Billund from Brussels, Amsterdam, Stockholm, Paris and Frankfurt. **New Air** (UK tel: 0161-489 2802) operates flights to Billund

Danish postboxes have a distinctive rounded top and bright red livery

DIRECTORY

from Birmingham, Manchester,
Bergen and Stavanger.
Flights from several European
cities go to Denmark's other
airports – from Amsterdam,
Berlin, Budapest and Oslo to
Aalborg and from Brussels,
Dusseldorf, Frankfurt,
Gothenburg, Manchester and
Stockholm to **Århus**. You can
fly to **Esbjerg** with Business Air
(UK tel: 0500 340 146) from
Aberdeen, East Midlands,
Edinburgh and Manchester.
Flight time from London to
Copenhagen is under two
hours. Flights also go to
Copenhagen from Aberdeen,
Birmingham, Dublin,
Edinburgh, Glasgow and
Manchester.
Kastrup airport is large and
modern with excellent shops,
including duty-free; it is 6 miles
(10km) southeast of
Copenhagen, with a frequent
bus service to Copenhagen
Central station. **Billund** airport
is smaller, just over a mile
(2km) from the town and within
walking distance of Legoland.
Århus airport (Tirstrup) also
operates a bus service to Århus

Denmark is a seafaring nation

bus station, 22 miles (35km)
away. **Esbjerg** airport is 6 miles
(10km) northeast of Esbjerg,
just off the E20.
Several airlines, including SAS
and Maersk, reduce their fares
in the summer months, when
fewer business travellers fly.

By Rail
Trains run direct to Denmark
from Germany, crossing the
border at Padborg and Rødby
(by ferry). International through
trains operate from Sweden,
Norway and Britain via ferries
(see below). From London, go
by train to Dover or Harwich,
and cross to Ostend or the
Hook of Holland and then by
train to Denmark. More
information from Wasteels
Travel (tel: 0171 834 7066).

By Ferry
Denmark has numerous ferry
connections with other north
European countries.
Scandinavian Seaways (in
Britain, tel: 0117 944 4723 for a
brochure; 01255 241 234 to
make a booking) operates one

service from Harwich to
Esbjerg, which takes about
20 hours. There are three to four
sailings a week, all year. A
special boat train,
'*Englænderen*' runs from
Esbjerg to Copenhagen. There
are many crossings from
Germany, Sweden and Norway,
and a few from Iceland, Poland
and Lithuania – details can be
found in the *Motoring Map, Ferry
Guide and Attractions* published
by the Danish Tourist Board.
Some ferry companies offer
discounts at certain times of the
year, and circular tour tickets
may be available on domestic
and international routes.

By Road
The motorway border crossing
between Germany and
Denmark is at Frøslev; there
are other road crossings
located at Kruså, Rudbøl, Sæd,

*It is often difficult to decide whether
the transport is a train or a bus*

Padborg and Møllehus.
Two coach companies run trips
from Britain to Denmark.
Eurolines (tel: 01582 404511),
the international arm of National
Express buses, goes five times
a week to Copenhagen via
Køge and four times a week to
Hirtshals via Århus and Aalborg,
using two different channel
routes – Dover to Calais with
P&O European Ferries, and
Ramsgate to Ostend with Sally
Line. **BB Travel** (tel: 0171-734
7998) goes twice a week to
Copenhagen, via Århus and
Odense using the P&O Dover to
Calais route. Journeys take
about 24 hours, longer from
Ramsgate.

Entry Formalities
All visitors to Denmark need a
valid passports which must
have at least two months to run
from the date they leave
Denmark. No visa is required
for residents of the UK, Canada,
USA or EU countries.

DIRECTORY

Beaches

Denmark's coastline, including all its islands, totals about 4,600 miles (7,400km), which means a lot of beaches. Most are sandy and backed by dunes. Few are 'developed' in the Mediterranean sense, but many have basic facilities. By the end of 1995, nearly 170 Danish beaches had been awarded the **Blue Flag** for clean and unpolluted beaches by the European Environmental Campaign.

The wide, white beaches on the west coast of **Jutland** form one of the longest stretches of sand – at Blokhus, for example, cars can be driven on to the beach. This coast does face the North Sea, though, which can make it cold, rough and windy. Few beaches are rocky or with cliffs, but dunes, especially in north and west Jutland, make varied coastal contours.

Calmer conditions and shallower waters prevail on Jutland's east coast, and on the east coasts of Funen, Falster and Langeland. On **Funen**, the best beaches are west of Bogense and along the northeast coast as far as Nyborg. The most pleasant of **Zealand's** beaches are on the north and southwest coasts. Islands with lovely beaches include Fanø and Bornholm. The keen-eyed may find fossils (on Mørs or Fur), and look out for amber.

Bathing is prohibited at a few harbours, identified by the flying of danger flags.

Topless bathing is allowed on all, and nude bathing on some beaches.

Camping and Caravanning

There are over 500 campsites in Denmark, in the countryside, near the towns and on the coast. All the sites are classified and given star ratings from one to five. One-star sites provide minimum sanitary installations and drinking water; three-star sites have showers, shaving points, laundry facilities and shops, while five-star sites have higher standards. The price depends on the classification. Many sites are well laid out in pleasant locations. Some have shops, a few have pools.

Spending the night in a car, tent, dormobile or mobile home on land outside an official site without the landowner's permission is forbidden, as is camping in car parks or laybys – and people parking on sand dunes or beaches are fined on the spot.

Foreign visitors should get a **Camping Card International** before they leave home. Otherwise, they can buy a pass at their first site, which is then valid for all approved campsites in Denmark. (See also page 98.)

The official guide to sites, *Camping Danmark,* can be obtained for a small fee from Campingrådet, Hesseløgade 16, DK-2100, Copenhagen Ø (tel: 39 27 88 41).

Many Danish campsites have static caravans or cabins for rent, usually available only on a weekly basis, from a Saturday. They are normally fully equipped except for bed linen.

Chemists see Pharmacies

Pleasure craft from the humblest...

Crime

Denmark is a very safe country, but you should not take any risks. When parking your car, make sure that it is locked and that no valuables or luggage are visible. It is unwise to wander around Christiania, in Copenhagen, at night, but mostly the rest of the city and other large towns are perfectly safe.

Customs Regulations

Visitors can bring in cars, motorcycles, caravans and boats, free of duty, but they must not lend them to Danish residents or accept payment for transporting people in them. All personal articles and meat, dairy products and vegetables for your own consumption can also be imported duty-free. The maximum amount of fish or shellfish which may be imported is 40lbs (18kg) per

person, and some species must be already gutted and cleaned. Apart from the usual restrictions on the importation of tobacco, alcohol and perfume by people aged 17 and over, Denmark also has strict rules about importing tea and coffee. There are no restrictions on the import or export of Danish or foreign currency.

Disabled Travellers

Denmark's provision for handicapped people is excellent. A comprehensive booklet *Access in Denmark – a travel guide for the disabled* is available from the Danish Tourist Board. It gives a comprehensive list of accessible places for wheelchair users, including facilities on trains, ferries and at airports, accommodation, and parking distances from museums. Wheelchairs can be hired on a daily or weekly basis (tel: 45 36 46 99 31).

DIRECTORY

Driving

Driving in Denmark is a pleasure as the roads are well maintained and traffic is light. Drivers who want to go on more scenic routes should follow the **Marguerit-rute** (Marguerite Route), along 2,100 miles (3,500km) of roads, following the road signs which feature a yellow flower on a brown background. Maps are on sale at tourist offices and Statoil service stations.

Be careful when turning left: road signs indicating places on the left are occasionally set on the lefthand side of the road, only at the junction itself, and not in advance. Motorways, which are toll-free, are often only two lanes in each direction, and have few service stations. Be careful when turning right in towns as a cycle track often runs between the pavement and the road; drivers must give way to cyclists who may be going straight on.

The minimum age for drivers is 18. Foreign cars must display a nationality plate and carry a warning triangle. (See also **Documents**, opposite.)

Accidents and Breakdowns

If you have an accident, phone 112 for the emergency services. Emergency phones are installed on motorways. If you break down, **Falck** the rescue service (tel: 70 10 20 30); operates a 24-hour service for which you will have to pay. If your car cannot be fixed on the spot it will be towed to a garage, but if you can get your car to a garage yourself, do so.

...to the highest can be seen here

You will have to pay VAT (currently 25 per cent) for materials and labour on the repair. (See also **Motoring Organisations**, below.)

Alcohol
There are strict penalties for motorists who drink and drive: it is best not to do so.

Car Rental
This is widely available from large international or smaller local companies, but it can be cheaper to book it in advance in your own country. By law you must be 20 years old to hire a car, but some companies do not accept drivers under 25.

Documents
If driving your own car, you will need to take your (valid) UK or EU driving licence and the car's registration papers. A Green Card is not compulsory, and you should check with your insurance company whether you need to take out any extra insurance.

Fuel
Petrol is sold in litres, often in self-service garages (*tank selv* or *selvbetjening*). Two grades of leaded petrol are sold – super benzine 98 octane, and low-lead 96 octane – and three grades of unleaded (*blyfri*), sold in 92, 95 and 98 octanes. There are plenty of garages in Denmark but few on motorways. Some garages accept credit cards, and at some automatic pumps you feed in kroner notes (Dkk 50 and 100).

Lights
It is now compulsory to use dipped headlamps at all times,

even during daylight hours. The lights of Danish-registered cars are of a lower density than UK-registered vehicles, so drivers should dip their lights early on meeting oncoming vehicles. All drivers with assymetric headlights, such as on right-hand drive cars, must cover part of the headlamp glass with an opaque material or use beam deflectors, available from motorist shops or motoring organisations.

Motorcycles
Riders and passengers must wear helmets, and always use dipped headlights.

Motoring Organisations
Forenede Danske Motorjere – **FDM** (Federation of Danish Motorists) does not provide a breakdown service, but offers legal and technical help to members of motoring organisations such as the British AA, which are affiliated to the AIT (Alliance Internationale de Tourisme). Their head office is at Firskovvej 32, PO Box 500, DK-2800, Lyngby (tel: 45 27 07 07).

Parking
In some towns with a car park you have to buy a parking ticket and display it: *parkeringsbillet påkrævet* means that a pay-and-display ticket is compulsory. In other towns, parking is free but you must display a parking disc which resembles a clock, and set the hands to the nearest quarter-hour following your arrival time. Signs such as *1 time, 2 timer* mean that you can park for one or two hours. Discs are available from tourist offices, garages, post offices,

DIRECTORY

police stations and some banks. *Parkering forbudt* means no parking, though you are allowed three minutes to pick up or drop off passengers. Parking meters must be fed on weekdays (09.00–18.00hrs) and Saturdays (09.00–13.00hrs). *Stopforbud* means no stopping.

Seat Belts
It is compulsory for drivers and passengers over 15 years of age to wear seat belts if they are fitted. Children under 3 years must be seated in a restraint system.

Speed Limits
On motorways the maximum speed is 68mph (110kph); other roads 50mph (80kph) and in built-up areas 30mph (50kph). The maximum speed on motorways for cars towing a caravan or trailer is 44mph (70kph).

Traffic Regulations
Drive on the right, overtake on the left. Most signs are international, but when you emerge from a side road on to a main road there is often a line of white triangles ('sharks' teeth') painted on the surface: this means that the traffic on the main road has right of way. You must not turn right at red lights unless a green arrow shows.
For several offences, including speeding, you can be fined on the spot and if you cannot pay, your car may be impounded.

Electricity
The electric current is 220 volts AC (50Hz) and sockets are of the two-point continental type. You will need an adaptor for appliances from the UK and a voltage transformer for appliances from the US or Canada.

Embassies and Consulates
United Kingdom
Embassy
40 Kastelsvej, DK-2100, Copenhagen, (tel: 35 26 46 00; fax: 31 58 10 12).

Consulates
Esbjerg, Fredericia, Herning, Odense, Rønne (Bornholm), Åbenra, Aalborg and Århus

Australia
Embassy
21 Kristianiagade, DK-2100, Copenhagen, (tel: 35 26 22 44; fax: 35 43 22 18).

Canada
Embassy
1 Kristen Bernikowsgade DK-1105, Copenhagen K, (tel: 33 12 22 99; fax: 33 14 05 85).

Republic of Ireland
Embassy
Østbanegade 21, DK-2100, Copenhagen, (tel: 31 42 32 33; fax: 35 43 18 58).

USA
Embassy
24 Dag Hammarskjölds Alle, DK-2100, Copenhagen, (tel: 31 42 31 44; fax: 35 43 02 23).

Emergency Telephone Numbers
Dial 112 for police, fire or ambulance services.
Emergency calls are free from public telephone boxes.

Entertainment

For big cities, the most up-to-date information is in *Copenhagen This Week* and *Whats On in Århus*, both of which are published monthly and available free from tourist offices, hotels and airports. Many other towns produce leaflets about local events, available from the same places.

Health

In the case of sudden illness or an accident, all visitors are entitled to free medical treatment in hospital. If you need a doctor for a non-urgent case ask your hotel or campsite warden to phone for you: an answer-phone service refers callers to a 'doctor on duty' service and each town has its own phone number.
British citizens should get booklet **T5**, *Health Advice for Travellers Anywhere in the World,* from post offices. Fill in both forms at the back of the leaflet and get them stamped at a post office, then take form E111 with you to Denmark. If you do receive medical treatment and the Danish doctor insists on cash, make sure you get a receipt. If you consult a doctor or dentist within the Danish Public Health Service, and show your passport or E111, the full costs of the medical consultation and part of the dental fee will be refunded if you take your receipts to the local council (*amtskommune*). In the Copenhagen area, the equivalent is the *magistrat*, and around Frederiksberg, the *kommunalbestyreise* (municipal administration). If you are

Entertainment may be innovative

prescribed any medicines, you must pay the first Dkk 800, which is not refundable. You can find out about doctors and dentists from the local *social-og sundhedsforvaltning* (social and health authority).

Holidays

On these days, all banks, businesses and shops are closed: New Year's Day, Maundy Thursday, Good Friday, Easter Monday, Great Prayer Day (fourth Friday after Good Friday), Ascension Day, Whit Monday, Constitution Day (5 June, from noon), Christmas Day, Boxing Day.
School summer holidays run between approximately 20 June and mid-August.

Lost Property

In Copenhagen you can try the following phone numbers, depending on where you lost your belongings: **aeroplane** – tel: 32 32 32 60; **bus** – tel: 36 45 45 45; **train** – tel: 36 44 20 10; **police** – tel: 31 74 88 22, or visit

DIRECTORY

Slotsherrensvej 113, DK-2720, Vanløse 2.

For lost **credit cards**, tel: 44 89 25 00. American Express tel: 80 01 00 21; Diners Club tel: 36 72 36 72; others tel: 44 89 25 00. For the **local police** in Copenhagen, tel: 31 74 88 22; in Århus, tel: 86 13 30 00.

Media

Radio Denmark broadcasts a five-minute English news bulletin at 08.31hrs, Monday to Friday, on Programme 3 (93.8MHz). English newspapers are on sale in Copenhagen and other large towns.

Money Matters

The currency is the Danish crown, *Krone* (Dkk), made up of 100 *øre*. *Kroner* come in notes of 50, 100, 500 and 1,000, and in coins of 1, 2, 5, 10, and 20; there are also coins of 25 and 50 *øre*. Travellers' cheques and Euro-cheques can be exchanged for Danish currency. Cash dispensers (called *Kontanten*) will give you Danish currency if you insert your credit card (Visa, MasterCard etc) or foreign curency notes.

The white cliffs of Møn (see page 86)

Banks charge a flat rate of commission for exchanging travellers' cheques and foreign currency, which may be very high and differs from bank to bank. Danish banks may refuse to exchange foreign bank notes of high denominations.

Credit cards (MasterCard, Visa) and charge cards (American Express and Diners Club) are widely accepted in shops, restaurants, hotels and garages in large towns, but may not be accepted in rural areas.

Opening Times

Banks
Open Monday to Friday only, 09.30–16.00hrs; on Thursdays open until 18.00hrs, though this can vary outside Copenhagen. In Copenhagen, outside banking hours, you can use 24-hour currency exchange machines at Unibank (4A Vesterbrogade in Axelborg Bldg, 35 Vimmelskaftet on Strøget, and 2A Vesterbrogade) and at Jyske Bank, 9 Vesterbrogade, near the Station. (See Money Matters.)

Shops
Shopping hours vary from town to town. Shops in Copenhagen and other large towns open Monday to Saturday at 10.00hrs, and close 17.30hrs; 19.00hrs or 20.00hrs Friday and 13.00hrs or 14.00hrs on Saturday, except for the first and last Saturday each month when they stay open until 16.00 or 17.00hrs.

Elsewhere, shops open Monday to Saturday, any time between 09.00 and 10.00hrs.

Closing hours and Saturday opening are much the same as in Copenhagen. New shopping laws allow shops to open 06.00–20.00hrs seven days a week, but few keep such long hours. Sunday opening is forbidden for department stores and other large shops. However, kiosks and small shops selling flowers, bread, *smørrebrød* and sweets may open. Petrol stations also open on Sunday and these sell quite a wide range of goods. In Copenhagen, the supermarket at the railway station is open until late and all day Sunday.

Museums, Churches etc
If you want to see a particular museum, check the opening times with the tourist office or museum itself. In Copenhagen and many other towns, most museums are open on Sundays and closed on Mondays.

The story is different, however, with more seasonal outdoor entertainment, which may be open seven days a week, for very long hours in mid-summer (such as Tivoli, Legoland and some folk museums), but they may only be open during the summer months.

Manor houses may be open in summer months only and perhaps only on certain days.
Churches are open for some hours most days, but may not welcome sightseers on Sundays.

Tourist Offices
The Copenhagen office at Tivoli is open seven days a week, May to mid-September, but the hours vary. In July and August,

it is open 08.00–23.00hrs. In May, June and the first half of September, it is open from 09.00–21.00hrs. The rest of the year open Monday to Friday 09.00–17.00hrs, Saturday 09.00–14.00hrs and closed on Sundays. Times vary in other towns.

Personal Safety
Always make sure your money, passport and travel documents are safe – in your hotel, on your person or in your car. (See also **Crime**.)

Pharmacies
The *Apotek* (chemist's shop) usually occupies a prime site in town and their opening hours are the same as other shops, but those in larger cities may stay open 24 hours a day. Pharmacies are the only places which sell medicines. If you regularly take a prescribed medicine, make sure you do not run out of it while you are in Denmark as chemists dispense prescriptions from Scandinavian doctors only. Preparations which are readily available over the counter in the UK may be on prescription only in Denmark.
Information leaflets issued by local tourist offices often carry the address and phone number of the pharmacy. (See also **Health**.)

Places of Worship
The state religion is Protestant, and church services are held on Sundays. Some Copenhagen churches, including St Alban, the Pentecostal Church and the International Baptist Church, hold services in English. Buddhists, German Evangelicals, Jehovah's Witnesses, Jews, Muslims, Quakers, Roman Catholics and Seventh Day Adventists will all find places of worship in Copenhagen. More information from *Copenhagen This Week*. In the rest of the country, Protestantism prevails.

Post Offices
In general, post offices open daily (except Sunday) from 09.00hrs or 10.00–17.00hrs. On Saturday those that open at all close at about noon. The post office at Copenhagen Central railway station opens daily on weekdays 08.00–22.00hrs, Saturday 09.00–16.00hrs, and Sunday 10.00–17.00hrs.

Public Transport
Denmark has an efficient public transport system of trains, buses and ferries. All timetables are coordinated so that no vehicle departs until the expected one arrives.

Air
Copenhagen is not only the hub of international routes, but also of domestic ones. Air fares from overseas to Danish regional airports may cost the same as flights to Copenhagen. Three airlines fly to regional airports – SAS, Maersk and Cimber Air – and offer a 10 per cent discount to those over 65 on some internal flights. From Roskilde, an air taxi flies to islands Anholt and Laesø.

Rail
The state railway system (**DSB** – Danske Statsbaner) operates

most trains, but some lines are still privately run (the one to Skagen, for example) and do not accept all tickets, such as Inter-Rail and Scanrail.

Lyn provide fast and comfortable long-distance travel throughout the country, but their coverage is somewhat limited. Newspapers, refreshments and payphones are available; seats (first and second class) must be reserved.

IC Intercity trains (first and second class) run more frequently, often an hourly service between main towns. Seat reservations are compulsory on trains crossing the Great Belt.

Danish Railways accepts **rail passes** as long as they have been bought outside Denmark. **Scanrail** is valid in Norway, Sweden and Finland, as well as Denmark for 5, 10, 21 days or for one month, and **Inter-Rail 26+** is valid for travelling in 19 European countries for 15 days or one month. Another option is a **Freedom Pass** for unlimited travel in one country only (on sale in 25 countries), and valid for 3, 5, or 10 days' travel within a month.

The country is divided into different zones, and ticket prices are based on the distance travelled; for longer journeys the cost per zone is reduced. You cannot easily break a journey as a time limit is set for the number of zones you are crossing. For example, a 3-zone ticket is valid for one hour, a 7-zone one for 2 hours. A 24-hour ticket is available that covers all zones.

Discounts are available for three or more adults travelling together. Children under the age of four go free at all times; those between four and eleven travel at half the adult fare.

An integrated transport system operates on S-trains, DSB/State and privately operated railways and on buses in the Metropolitan (HT) area of Copenhagen and North Zealand. So for a trip to Elsinore, for example, which may also include a bus ride, you only need to buy one ticket.

The graceful curve of the longboat is reflected in the longhouse

Model ships hang in many of Denmark's churches

Luggage trolleys are available at some stations, for which a charge may be made (a lock system operates at Copenhagen's main station, København H, for which you currently require a Dkk10 coin) but is refundable when the trolley is returned. Left luggage offices exist at some stations. (See also page 26.)

Buses

Not many long-distance buses operate in Denmark, but the fares are lower than on trains. Buses are the only option in Funen and northeast Jutland. Local buses are modern and comfortable. Each town sets its own basic ticket price, and the more tickets you buy, the less each journey costs. Some towns offer special rates to tourists, notably Odense and Århus.

Ferries

About 80 ferry services sail from Danish harbours, more frequently in summer than in winter. If you have a car, the cost of your journey depends on the number of passengers; foot passengers pay less. If your train or bus journey includes a ferry crossing, this is covered in the ticket price. On busy routes (the Great Belt ferry and Rødby to Puttgarden) and on summer weekends, it is sensible to book in advance. The Danish Tourist Board publishes a *Motoring Map* which includes a ferry guide, giving fares and frequency of sailings to and within Denmark.

Senior Citizens

Men and women who receive an old age pension in their own country are entitled to reduced train fares in Denmark. British travellers aged 65 and over, who already have a Senior Railcard, should then buy a Rail Europe Senior Card in the UK. This must be produced when buying a Danish train ticket. Discounts are available every day except Fridays, Sundays, Bank Holidays and the preceeding day (see page 117), and for 12 days around Christmas and New Year. There are no discounts for bus travel.

Student and Youth Information

Reduced train fares are available for young people aged 12 to 25 holding Eurail passes (only on sale outside Europe), Inter-Rail passes (available on a zonal basis for under-26s – Denmark is grouped with Austria, Switzerland and Germany), Freedom passes and Scanrail passes (see page 121). At the main railway station in Copenhagen, the **Inter-Rail Centre** offers the younger traveller information, a free shower, and refreshments (open daily 07.00hrs to midnight, June to September). Accommodation in summer is provided at an **InterPoint Centre**, run by the YMCA and TWCA at 15 Valdemarsgåde (tel: 31 31 15 74).

In Copenhagen the **Use-It Youth Information Centre** (13 Rådhusstræde, tel: 33 15 65 18) is open daily from mid-June to mid-September, 09.00–19.00hrs (rest of year Monday to Friday, 10.00–16.00hrs). This centre helps young people find cheap accommodation and restaurants. Use-It also sorts out young people's travel problems, stores luggage (free), and makes contact between drivers and hitch-hikers leaving Copenhagen. It also produces an annual English language publication *Playtime*.

There are four large hostels in and around Copenhagen, called **Sleep-Ins**, which are open for some months between May and September and provide cheap bed and breakfast. The most central is in Absalonsgade (tel: 31 31 20 70); the others are in Frederiksberg to the west (tel: 35 36 60 16), in Blegdamsvej, east of the centre (tel: 35 26 50 59) and at Ishøj about 6 miles (10km) south (tel: 43 73 40 83). **Cab-Inn Hotels**, (in Esbjerg too), offer cheap rooms (tel: 35 36 11 11).

Taxis

Recognisable by the green *TAXA* (taxi) sign on its roof and the illuminated *fri* (free) sign in the front windscreen, taxis are an expensive way to travel, but there are plenty of them in main towns. Taxis are metered and the tip is included in the price.

Useful Dialling Codes from Denmark to:
Australia 00 61
Canada 00 1
Ireland 00 353
UK 00 44
US 00 1
Always follow the above with the area code (minus the initial zero), then the number. The international dialling code for Denmark from Australia is 0011 45; from Ireland 00 45; from the UK 00 45; from the US and Canada 011 45 .

Telephones

Danish public telephones work efficiently both for national and international calls, but some phones do not refund your money if the call is not answered. The best way round this problem is to insert the fewest number of coins necessary, or to make more than one call at a time.

For internal calls, lift the receiver, put in a Dkk 1 coin and wait for the dialling tone; for long-distance calls, put in at least Dkk 5 or 10. On newer telephones, dial the number first and insert coins only when the phone rings. For more information about **long-distance** calls, tel: 141; to **reverse the charges**, tel: 115; for **information**, tel: 118. There are no area codes in Denmark – just dial the eight numbers. At Copenhagen main railway station there is a Telecom Centre which provides the user full office facilities.

Time

Denmark is on Central European Time (GMT+1),

A wonderful view from Frøbjerg Hill, Funen

which is one hour ahead of Britain, 6 hours ahead of New York, 9 hours behind Sydney and 11 hours behind New Zealand. Summer Time (GMT+2) is observed from the last Sunday in March to the last Saturday in September.

Tipping
Tipping does not exist in Denmark.

Toilets
Usually indicated by a pictograph, or marked WC, *toiletter*, or *Damer/Herrer*, public toilets are clean – and they are usually free.

Tourist Offices
The Danish Tourist Board (DTB) in the UK (which also serves Ireland), is at 55 Sloane Street, London SW1X 9SY (tel: 0171-259 5959, from 11.00–16.00hrs, Monday to Friday). In the USA, the DTB is at 655 Third Avenue, 18th Floor, New York, NY 10017 (tel: 212/949 2333).
In Denmark, *turistinformationen* (tourist offices) are generally centrally situated and well signed (a white letter *i* on a green background). Staff are helpful and speak several languages.

LANGUAGE

Danish is a Germanic language, close to Swedish and Norwegian, and many words are similar to German. But it is a difficult language to pronounce because some letters (d, g) are silent in the middle or at the end of words, h before a v becomes silent, and some specifically Scandinavian vowels (æ, ø, å), are awkward to say correctly. But the Danes are aware of this problem and most speak very good English.

The following words should help you to get around and read menus (which are often also in English and German).

yes ja
no nej
please vær så venlig
thank you tak
hello hej
goodbye farvel
good morning godmorgen
good afternoon goddag
good evening godaften
good night godnat

entrance indgang
no entry ingen adgang
  (for pedestrians)
exit udgang
no exit ingen udgang
emergency exit nødudgang
push/pull skub/træk or
  tryk/træk
ladies damer
gentlemen herrer
toilets toiletter
open åben
closed lukket
no smoking rygning forbudt
arrival ankomst
departure afgang
timetable køreplan

townplan bykort
step down/up trin ned /op
no standing rejs Dem ikke op

Monday mandag
Tuesday tirsdag
Wednesday onsdag
Thursday torsdag
Friday fredag
Saturday lørdag
Sunday søndag

1 en
2 to
3 tre
4 fire
5 fem
6 seks
7 syv
8 otte
9 ni
10 ti

opening times åbningstider
o'clock klokken
exhibition udstilling
do not touch må ikke berøres
petrol benzin
car bil
railway station banegård
railway line jernbane
street gade
ferry færge
no entry (cars) ingen indkørsel
Great Britain Storbritannien
USA De Forenede Stater

Food
breakfast morgenmad
lunch frokost
dinner middagsmad
starters forretter
soups supper
main courses hovedretter
fish dishes fiskeretter
cold dishes fra det kolde
  køkken
hot dishes fra det varme
  køkken

LANGUAGE

baked bagt	**vegetables** grøntsager
roast helstegt, steg	**peas** ærter
steamed dampet	**potatoes** kartofler
smoked røget	**cheese** ost
pork flæsk, svine	**fruit salad** frugtsalat
chicken kylling	
boiled chicken høne/hønse	**coffee/tea** kaffe/the
white bread franskbrød	**house wine** husets vin
rye bread rugbrød	**red/white** rød/hvid
French bread flûte	**apple juice** æblemost
Danish pastry Wienerbrød	**orange juice** appelsinjuice
butter smør	**full cream milk** sødmælk
shellfish skaldyr	**semi-skimmed milk** letmælk
herring sild	**skimmed milk** skummetmælk
trout ørred	
cod torsk	*The Tycho Brahe Planetarium,*
shrimps rejer	*Copenhagen*

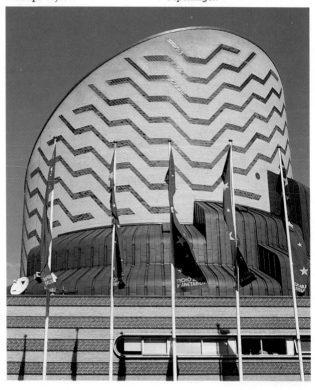

INDEX/ACKNOWLEDEMENTS

Acknowledgements

The Automobile Asociation wishes to thank the following photographers and libraries for their assistance in the preparation of this book:

DEREK FORSS took all the photographs and cover (©AA PHOTO LIBRARY) except:

AA PHOTO LIBRARY (Jesper Westley Jorgensen) 4 Boat in marina, 20 Statue of Hans Christian Andersen, 58 Skagen
J ALLAN CASH PHOTOLIBRARY 57 Silkeborg Lakes
THE DANISH TOURIST BOARD 7 Elderly Dane (Somer), Dane (Carrebye), 11 Fanø toddler (Nebbia), 42 Æroskøbing (Pressehuset), 71 Samsø (Sommer), 83 Kalundborg (Lennard), 89 Rebild Hills (Sommer), 117 entertainment (Johnsen)
MARY EVANS PICTURE LIBRARY 6 The Emperor's New Clothes
NATURE PHOTOGRAPHERS LTD 87 Red-backed shrike (Kevin Carlson)
JUDITH SAMSON 61 Windmill at Skagen
SPECTRUM COLOUR LIBRARY 25 the Bazarbygningen, 27 Town Hall Square, 69 Old Town Museum
ZEFA PICTURES LTD 41 Langeland

Contributors for this revision:
Copy editor: Hilary Hughes; **Verifier**: Judith Samson

The Automobile Association also wishes to thank the **Forenede Danske Motorjere (FDM)** for their assistance in updating the Directory section for this revision.